Effective Coaching

Lessons from the coaches' coach

Second Edition

Myles Downey

THOMSON

TM

TEXERE

Australia · Canada · Mexico · Singapore · Spain · United Kingdom · United States

THOMSON

Effective Coaching:
Lessons from the Coaches' Coach, Second Edition
Myles Downey

Copyright © 2003 by Myles Downey

Forward © 2003 by W. Timothy Gallwey

First published in 1999 by Orion Business.

Fully revised second edition published in 2003 by TEXERE, an imprint of Thomson Business and Professional Publishing, a part of the Thomson Corporation. Thomson, the Star logo, TEXERE, and Thomson Business and Professional Publishing are trademarks used herein under license.

Printed and bound in the United States of America.
ISBN 1-58799-172-1
2 3 4 5 6 7 09 08 07 06 05 04

For more information, contact TEXERE at Thomson Higher Education, 5191 Natorp Boulevard, Mason, OH 45040, USA. Or you can visit our website at www.thomson.com/learning/texere.

A CIP catalogue record for this book is available from the British Library.

Effective Coaching

Contents

Acknowledgements

Many people have contributed to my being able to write this book. There have been coaches, mentors, teachers and professional friends and colleagues who have helped me learn over a period of more than twenty years. And then all the people I have coached or trained to coach: I particularly thank Alan Fine, Graham Alexander, Martin Brooks, Sir John Whitmore, Susie Morell, Ben Cannon, Caroline Harris, Charles Sherno, Chris Morgan, Tony Morgan and Philip Goldman. Since the first edition, I have learned so much more, as I hope this new book demonstrates, and my colleagues on the faculty team at The School of Coaching have each made a significant contribution: Jane Meyler, Charles Brook, Judith Firman, Sheridan Maguire, Anne Scoular, Dr Mike Turner, Trevor Waldock and David Webster. I also extend my gratitude to Barry Curnow and Naona Beecher-Moore for their personal and professional support. A word for Cliff Kimber for reading the first drafts of this book and for all the advice, suggestions and support. Thanks too to David Wilson of TEXERE for his sensitivity to this material, for his ability to translate it into practice and thus for helping me write a better book. A final word of thanks goes to Tim Gallwey for writing *The Inner Game of Tennis*, a book that opened up a new world for me.

Myles Downey

Foreword

What is this thing that we call coaching? And who gets to say?

We are witnessing the emergence of a new profession called 'coaching in business and in life'. Though coaching in sports has a long heritage, executive coaching, manager as coach, and life coaching are new means by which people are helping other people professionally. Ironically, the business coaching profession has learned much from sports coaching and is, in turn, exploring approaches which could come full circle and end up transforming traditional sports coaching.

What is interesting about the beginning of any new profession is that agreed upon definitions, practices and boundaries do not exist. People who coach and people who are coached don't really know exactly what it is that is happening. The shared understanding of the distinctions between coaching and its siblings: managing, consulting, leadership and teaching are anything but crisp.

At this early stage in the evolution of the profession some people will call themselves business coaches simply by self-declaration. It is no more complicated than printing up a business card and a brochure. Then some of these coaches will get together and decide that it is up to them to define what coaching is and what it is not. Soon thereafter they will want to enlarge their authority to embrace the right to certify – to decide on the criteria by which someone may or may not legitimately call themselves a coach.

There is a somewhat disturbing question about this process. Who is to certify the certifiers? Human beings in the absence of authority are curious creatures. Actually we are at that moment perhaps at our most human. But, almost immediately, uncomfortable with the apparent uncertainty, we rush to establish authority, and risk in the process the loss of a portion of our humanity. The haste to establish authority could be called a doubting of the evolutionary process of things. But with coaching there is an inherent difference from most other professions. If the result of coaching is a high level of performance – the winning of a game or the achievement of a business or life goal – it is not the coach who can win, but the individual or team being coached. The coach cannot kick a goal or prevent one from being scored. The coach cannot run the race, meet the quota, achieve the bottom line, or design the product. In spite of the fact that the coach does not set foot on the playing field, he or she is often paid high wages for the perceived impact on individual and team performance.

The fact that a coach's effectiveness is measured by the success of those he or she coaches points to an inherent difference in this new profession. Not only is there no established body of knowledge called coaching, but the coach often has less expertise than the one being coached. The coach does not need to impart knowledge, advice, or even wisdom. What he or she must do is speak, and act, in such a way that others learn and perform at their best.

It is thus an indirect profession. It is an evocative profession. To 'bring out the best in another individual or team' is a metaphor at best. Coaches cannot actually reach in and bring the best out of anyone but themselves. All that can be done is to say, be, and do and let the others respond with excellence or not. Those who are considered good coaches have a higher probability of seeing excellence emerge. But there is little explainable cause and effect in the matter.

So how are we really going to define the set of competencies that help another become what they can be? I would suggest that to do so prematurely would be a mistake. And doing so will make it more difficult, not easier, to coach successfully. The only authoritative person to certify a coach is the person or team being coached. They are in the best position to know the kind of impact that the coach has had on their learning, performance, and enjoyment at work and on the field. Whatever is decided about what coaching is or isn't, it is the end user that must decide if it was valuable.

Such a position is consistent with the nature of coaching, which amongst all forms of help is predicated on empowering the one being coached. The coach is the person who should be helping you to believe in yourself – to trust in yourself – and not in some external agency. And if a coach asks for trust, the only proper use of that trust given is to return it back doubly to the one being coached. The only authority a coach needs is the authority to say to another 'Trust thyself'.

The goal of coaching is to establish a firmer connection with an *inner* authority that can guide vision and urge excellence and discriminate wisdom without being subject to an 'inner bully', that has established its certification from external dictates and imposes them on you without your authority to do so.

This is not to say that the new profession does not need controls. Not at all. It needs controls precisely when it enters into the domain of other disciplines that require certification. Coaching is not therapy. Therapists do therapy and are required to meet certain qualifications to practice therapy. Coaching is not consulting and should not enter into that established domain of professional activity. And coaching is not religious or spiritual counseling. All of these may help people, but equally all of these are separate established activities that follow their own rules.

Coaching can't 'own' the broad activity called 'helping other people'. If it tries to cross into therapy and family or professional religious or spiritual counseling, then the instant it does so it is responsible to the rules of those established in those domains.

Until then, why not let those who can establish themselves as helpful to their clients define for themselves, and their clients, what coaching is, and by stated contract proceed on that basis? This will give coaching a chance to 'grow up' and to become what it is and can be, without the rush to dominate the emerging profession by some self-appointed authority.

It is up to the individual coach or coaching group, and indeed line-managers who adopt the core skills of coaching into their working practices, to provide to the client a description of their competencies and experience, their definition of coaching and the boundaries of coaching they will observe. Then it is up to the client to be the judge of the extent of helpfulness of that coach and whether or not to continue engaging the service.

I write this in this introduction because Myles Downey in his approach to coaching has attempted to preserve the integrity of 'coaching' as a discipline while offering clarity to its distinctiveness in the approach he calls 'Effective Coaching'. In the process of doing so, he rigorously resists anything that increases the coach's authority at the expense of that of the client individual or team being coached. His approach is true to the spirit and ethos of coaching in its purest sense. It can offer rich rewards to the person or team being coached and to the coach or line-manager who embrace his style and beliefs. When coaching is effective, it requires no additional authority from third parties.

W. Timothy Gallwey
25 July 2003

Introduction

Why rewrite a book that has been well received and continues to sell? There are many reasons. The truth, however, is very simple and in the end it comes down to one thing: I think coaching is important. And therefore I am determined to write the best book that I can. This means correcting the errors of the first version, incorporating the new thinking that has emerged, and integrating the experience I have gained since the first publication. This new version, therefore, brings together the research, lessons and insights of more than twenty years of coaching and of training others to coach.

Let me state why I think coaching is important. Coaching has the capacity to bring humanity back into the workplace. This is critical because much of what we are doing in the workplace – and beyond – has the effect of squeezing humanity out. The ever-increasing drive for efficiencies (not effectiveness, note), the restructuring, the re-engineering, the ever more stretching goals, the apparent expendability of the 'human resource', all these, unfettered, sap spirit, energy and creativity and thus impoverish the human being and the organisation in which they work. But even despite all that, if we are able to take the opportunity offered to us right now we will realise that we are perhaps on the brink of discovering the extraordinary benefits of letting humanity loose in the workplace – and beyond. When the whole human being, with all its capacities – intelligence, creativity, imagination, sensitivity and pragmatism to name but a few – freed from the tyranny of fear and doubt, expresses itself in the workplace, then extraordinary results accrue. Idealism? I hope so. But it is also the result of observation over many years. It is a simple notion: people work better, more productively, more effectively, more creatively when they are cared for. And caring means having the difficult conversations too. Pragmatism? Again, I hope so. For the goals of productivity and fulfilment are far from incompatible; the one feeds and supports the other. Coaching can tap into the resources of the whole human being, for the benefit of the individual employee and the organisation itself.

So the intent in writing and rewriting this book is to present a comprehensive introduction to coaching as it occurs in the workplace. To achieve this I have structured the book so that it moves from a conversation about what coaching is, and in particular what *effective coaching* is, to an introduction to the key models used in coaching, and a description of the core skills. The book then moves from a generic account of coaching into the more specific applications: where does coaching fit in the workplace? How might one get started? And what about coaching teams? The final chapter then broadens the outlook and suggests a need to consider any coaching intervention within its context: for instance, how does coaching an individual meet the needs of the organisation in which they work? A number of appendices are attached at the end. They contain information that does not obviously fit within the structure of the book but which is valuable. The book is intended to be very practical. It deals with real, day-to-day matters. It is full of anecdotes and outlines of conversations that will be familiar to anyone who has worked in an organisation. The aim is to show in a very recognisable context how coaching can be effective. For line-managers I hope this demonstrates that coaching is not an additional responsibility or chore but is part of the way in which the core job is delivered.

Since this book is about coaching in the workplace, I have in mind three particular target audiences: line-managers, professional coaches and internal change agents such as Human Resource specialists. For professional coaches and change agents, coaching is either the job itself or a significant part of it, so the relevance of this book is clear. Line-managers, whether they are the CEO or a supervisor on the shop-floor, do not always see that coaching is part of their role, or understand how it fits in. So I suggest here that coaching is a critical skill set that a line-manager needs to be equipped with in order to be effective. This idea is developed further in the book. Many line-managers have come to realise that the typical approaches to managing their teams and direct reports, such as 'command-and-control', are not only insufficient to the needs of the organisations for which they work (i.e. the staff are insufficiently productive or effective) but also not conducive to getting the best from their colleagues. Coaching, practised even moderately well, balanced with effective management and leadership, is a very big part of the solution.

The feedback from the first edition suggests that the ideas laid out here are applicable to anyone who has a responsibility or a desire to help others learn and perform effectively. So the readership net widens to include consultants, teachers, parents, sports coaches and many others. The primary aim of the book, as I have said, is to provide a comprehensive introduction to coaching. The secondary aim, which is more difficult to achieve, is to inspire people to take the opportunities that present themselves on a daily basis, a chance conversation in the corridor or a request for help with the homework, and to use the techniques presented here to make a difference for others. Life, and not just work-life, can and should be productive, fulfiling and a joy.

There are many changes in this new version of the book. The structure has been entirely reshaped, necessitating the rewriting of almost every page. There is new information and there are new models and insights. The most important addition, I believe, is Chapter 11 called 'Coaching in Context'. Let me explain. There is a tendency, in the literature and the practice of coaching, to view the individual being coached in isolation, and to work with that individual's perceptions and aspirations without referring to the context in which they are operating. An example of this is the habit amongst some professional coaches of referring to the person being coached as the client and of insisting that the coaching is entirely confidential. First, when the organisation is paying the coach, the organisation is the client; and secondly, the organisation has a responsibility to ensure that the outputs from the coaching intervention benefit the organisation. This means that a representative of the organisation should have some oversight of the coaching and input into the objectives for the intervention, so in this sense it is not entirely confidential. This new chapter is intended to provide a means of looking at and understanding the organisational context in which the individual being coached is working. This helps the individual see how their actions, and any changes they might make, may or may not contribute to the organisation's overall aims. Perhaps more importantly, it means that those things that might cause an individual to fail – the culture, conflicting strategic intents and the politics, for example – can also be accounted for and planned for.

There are a number of words or terms that I have used very deliberately in the book. You may already have noticed that I somewhat laboriously use the term 'line-manager' when 'manager' might appear to do just as well. I use this term for two reasons. First, I will argue later in the book that the line-manager's role is composed of three skill sets: leadership, management and coaching. To label the role 'manager' is to label it by a subset of the role, taking attention away from all it encompasses. Secondly, I want the term to embrace everyone in an organisation who has a direct reporting line to them; that is to say they are responsible for the leadership, management and coaching of others, from CEO to supervisor. To use the term 'manager' might be seen to suggest that only the beleaguered souls in the middle ranks of the organisation need coach.

I also somewhat unusually use the term 'player' to refer to the recipient of coaching when I am writing generically about coaching. 'Coachee' is the more common word but, in addition to the fact that it does not easily slip off the tongue, it puts the player in a passive, secondary position, at the butt of the person doing the coaching. The word 'player' gives primacy to the recipient and acknowledges the fact that it is they who will be performing whatever actions emerge from the coaching. There is one final reason: I like the idea that people might approach work with a positive and creative mindset, a certain playfulness, at least some of the time.

You may also note that in the text I refer to The Inner Game which is the name that Tim Gallwey uses to describe his books and his intellectual capital. When I mention his work, say a model or definition, I use capital letters to signify his authorship. When I go on to describe how The Inner Game plays out in coaching this is purely my own understanding. I would not want anyone having read those parts of this book to think that they now understood all of The Inner Game as Gallwey means it, nor think that this is the official Inner Game version of coaching.

I hope you enjoy reading the book and that you can easily translate the ideas into action.

Chapter 1

A conversation

'Henry! How are you?'

'God knows!'

'What do you mean?'

'I'm on autopilot. I've had about 17 hours sleep all week.'

Just so you, the reader, know, we are in the offices of Brand plc by the water-cooler on the fourth floor.

'Wow. How's that?'

'You don't want to know.'

'Try me.'

'How long do you have?'

'Seriously? About half an hour now, but if we need it I have an hour towards the end of the day, after 4.30.'

'Yea, maybe we should talk. We can sit over there.'

'Fine. Let me fill my glass. So … what's happening?'

'What it feels like is that I'm working flat out and getting nowhere.'

There's a pause. Melanie says nothing. Henry continues:

'You know I have an objective to develop our offering for the Public Sector?'

'Of course. We worked through it before.'

'It's become more complex since then.'

'In what way?'

'In how many ways more like. The people I'm working with are a bunch of half-wits for a start. Nothing that I ask them to do gets done, or if it does it's so bad that I have to re-do it myself. My own team is the worst, the guys from finance are just slow, but at least they get it done.'

'What else?'

'What else? Is that not enough for you?'

'Well, you said "complex" and while…'

'No, no, there's more. We made some assumptions about the costs at the very beginning and we tested them with a number of potential clients. Of course, what we did not anticipate was that the Government would stop funding centrally and require the departments to do this from their own budgets.'

'They still want it, the departments?'

'More then ever, as far as we can tell. They've just got less money.'

'What else?'

'Wh … Sorry. Stress. The really difficult bit is that our glorious leader, Steve, is breathing down our necks – my neck mostly – asking for one thing, and Jeremy from Marketing is asking for another with no less intensity.'

'What else?'

Henry shakes his head. Nothing.

'Then, if I have understood, there are three parts to this: the ability of the project team, a shift in the financial parameters, and the differing needs of our two friends, Steve and Jeremy.'

'That's right. Although, on the third point, it's as much about the pressure they put on me as it is about their "needs", as you put it?'

'OK. So four things then, including the pressure they are putting on you. Which would be most interesting to talk about first?'

'Sorting out the boys.'

'Steve and Jeremy. You're sure?'

'Yes, I think so.'

'It's just that the feedback from your team in the last 360, if you remember, suggested that you were overly controlling and unwilling to delegate. I'm just wondering if that's part of this?'

'Fair enough. I think I've been doing better on that since our last conversation – at least until this project got silly. I really think I need to sort the Steve and Jeremy issue first. If they let us get on with it we could sort the other things.'

'So tell me what's going on with them?'

'You know how it is where we sit, all open plan. Steve and Jeremy both have to walk through my area to get to their offices so they're forever "dropping in". That would be bad enough but they are both looking for different things. Steve wants us to cut this thing to the bare bones so that he can show the executive team how good he is at managing costs, and Jeremy wants this to be the sexiest thing ever, all bells and whistles, which he thinks will make it easier to sell, so that he can show the exec that he can bring our services to different markets. They are both leaning on me – and the others in the team – making demands that the other overturns. And since one of them is likely to be next Head of Division you don't want to upset either.'

'So how are you managing?'

'I guess we're just agreeing with both of them and hoping they don't notice. Other than that I just try and steer my way through.'

'What does that mean?'

'I make the best guess that I can – given the information – and make sure that I present it to them individually so that I can speak up the things that support their needs and conceal the things that don't. It's bloody exhausting.'

Henry starts laughing.

'What?'

'They never do notice. They're too busy playing politics to take the time to get inside the project.'

'What can you do? What options do you have?'

'If I thought I had options …'

'Jesus Henry, don't be so cantankerous.'

'Sorry. It's the stress. Again.'

'Tell me, in an ideal world how would things be different?'

There's a pause while Henry thinks.

'There would be a clear set of objectives that we had all agreed. That sounds so pathetic. You know there are objectives already. But Steve and Jeremy have not bought into them and they are now using the fact that there's a shift in the financing to bend things to their own ends.'

'So what do you need to do?'

'I need to get to a new set of objectives that account for the current situation and that all parties agree to.'

'How might you achieve that?'

'Arrange some kind of meeting. Although first I'd have to get marketing to complete the survey, then finance would have to cost the various options …'

'What are you thinking?'

'I said earlier that "I just try and steer my way through", but that's the wrong approach completely.'

'It is?'

'Of course. If I try and find a compromise I please no one. The other option, I've just realised, is to identify the various possibilities with the costings worked out and then to get Steve, Jeremy and the others to make a binding decision. We'd have to do it in a very pragmatic, business-like way so that the personal agendas were minimised.'

'So what needs to happen from here?'

'The first step is to get my own team on board so that we complete the survey and the costings exercise as quickly as possible.'

'But you said they weren't performing well.'

'I know. I was a bit unfair. It's impossible to perform well when the goal-posts keep moving and people change the rules. Plus, I think that the prospect of getting our two friends off our collective back will be so appealing that they'll pull out all the stops.'

'And then?'

'Then arrange a meeting at which we present the possibilities. We'd need to get Mac there as well. This could also solve the second issue – the fact that the source of funding has changed – because I'll have more people to help me work through.' (Mac is the current Head of Division.)

'How confident are you that this will work?'

'On a scale of one to ten, about an eight.'

'There were three, no four, issues at the beginning and it sounds like you've got some movement on three of them. What about the team/control matter?'

'I really do think that has shifted. And I also think that part of the problem was that we had conflicting objectives, caused by my own indecision and by Steve and Jeremy. The 360 will happen again in about three months, maybe we should look at it together then.'

'Fine.'

'Thanks, Melanie.'

COACHING

When we run workshops at The School of Coaching we nearly always start by getting someone from the group to come to the front and coaching them on a real, business issue. This is the best way I know of getting people to think about coaching, apart from which it can be fairly dramatic as the coaching is 'for real', it is not a role-playing exercise and there is no guarantee that it is going to work out. The conversation played out above is an example of the kind of issue that people bring to such sessions, although it is presented here in such a way that Melanie could be either Henry's line-manager, a colleague, an internal change agent or a professional coach from outside the organisation. At the end of the coaching demonstration we ask the other participants a simple question: 'What did you notice?'

Here are some typical responses:

'You really listened.'

'You asked a lot of questions.'

'You spent a lot of time trying to understand.'

'You summarised frequently.'

'You let him work it out for himself.'

'You added no value.'

'You did not add in anything, like suggestions or advice.'

'I had so many thoughts about what he should do.'

'What if the course of action they had decided on was wrong?'

'That was not coaching, it was more like counselling.'

'If I did that in my office they'd think I had gone mad.'

'In my country the manager has to know the answer or he'd lose credibility.'

'What happens if the course of action the person chooses is in opposition to the company's plans?'

'I just don't have the time to do that.'

People come to these workshops to discover about coaching. Their initial expectations are that it has something to do with passing on either knowledge, experience, expertise or wisdom or that it is in some sense an applied psychology, that there are techniques and tools that can be learned and then implemented to make people more motivated or whatever. What they actually discover, however, is that coaching is both less and more than that. In this book I will try to answer the questions raised above and to give a sense of the productivity, fulfilment and joy that can arise from effective coaching.

Chapter 2
Coaching described

The conversation in the previous chapter is a good example of effective coaching. The questions and objections listed reflect a general confusion about what coaching is, what its function is and how it fits in the workplace. In this chapter I want to bring some clarity to the 'territory' and to make a case for a particular approach. In doing this I will give a brief overview of the field, and bring particular attention to two congruent approaches, The Inner Game and non-directive coaching (the latter being the offspring of the former), and thus establish a foundation for the rest of the book. The question about how coaching fits in the workplace is addressed in Chapter 6.

THE TERRITORY AND THE CONFUSION

'Coaching is for failures.'
'Coaching is a mark of my status (the company pays for my executive coach).'

'Coaching is an emerging profession.'
'Coaching is a line-management competency.'

'Coaching is a fad.'
'Coaching can save the world.'

'Coaching is a second career' (soon to retire HR manager).

'Coaching is … not my job' (line-manager, coaching workshop).

Coaching means different things to different people depending on who they are, what they are doing and what their experience of coaching is. A Human Resource manager taking early retirement and thinking about how he might use the next stage of his life productively will have a very different perspective from the line-manager in an IT business who has just been told to attend a workshop on coaching skills – when what she really wants to do is to continue developing the software. There is no commonly held definition of coaching. In a way this is a good thing because definitions, while giving clarity, can also exclude other possibilities and make other notions, perhaps valuable ones, wrong.

If I tell someone that I am a coach, the immediate question is 'in what sport?'. For most people the initial exposure to coaching is through sport. Almost all sports coaching is built around the idea that coaching is essentially the transfer of knowledge. The coach is the expert, knows the correct technique and will tell you how to perform. As this knowledge/expert model is also the predominant model in our education systems, it is hardly surprising then that, in the world of work, people make similar assumptions about coaching.

The disciplines of psychology and psychotherapy offer another perspective on coaching, and indeed there is a point of view that only people with qualifications in one of the above should be allowed to coach. The conclusion of that argument can only be that we should all – managers, parents, teachers, spouses, partners, siblings, colleagues and friends – be trained therapists. Or cease talking to each other. Beacuse coaching is, in a sense, happening all the time; any time one person discusses with another how to do something – that's coaching. There is something about the first part of the 'conclusion' that I find appealing, and I don't deny that there are times when not talking would resolve many problems. But the reality, of course, is that neither 'solution' is practical. Silence may be golden but it would be very dull, and coaching is going on all around us – often with very beneficial results – and the world is not full of therapists (even though it might seem like it at times).

A range of other approaches to coaching have roots in the post-Maslow self-actualisation movement, such as Transformational Technology and Appreciative Enquiry, or hybrids – in this case with psychology – such as Neuro-Linguistic Programming. If you read around the territory for a while, you will also get to the pop-psychology, the self-help, the positive thinking and the religious schools. But it does not stop there. You can have Executive Coaching, Developmental Coaching, and Performance Coaching. Senior executives get coached because they do not have the time or inclination to go to the appropriate training programme. That is those, of course, who are willing to admit that they have something to learn.

And then there is Life Coaching. While I am sure that there are some life coaches out there doing good work in a responsible manner, there are also a lot of people doing the work of counsellors without anything like the appropriate training. I can also add counselling and mentoring (see Appendix 1). And the training itself contributes to the confusion. Training is available in coaching at almost every level in almost every form imaginable. At one extreme you can get a master's degree and at the other a distance learning programme: a couple of years' academic study or a couple of phone calls.

There is yet another approach to coaching. The principles upon which it is founded first came to prominence as The Inner Game, and have been developed by myself and others, particularly in the UK, as Non-Directive Coaching. One thing that makes this approach different is that it does not rely on the knowledge, experience, wisdom or insight of the coach but rather on the capacity of individuals to learn for themselves, to think for themselves and be creative. Just think of all the learning and creativity that has been lost in work organisation because a manager imposed his own solution on a colleague rather than asking a simple question such as 'What could you do?'. But I get ahead of myself.

Given all the different sources, inspirations and applications it is no wonder that there is confusion. It seems to me that one way of bringing clarity is to offer a proposition for *effective coaching*. You see, coaching is in danger of being defined by the inputs the philosophies, models and approaches that its champions bring with them, and not by the outputs: the results that we need in our places of work. Coaches are not retained by organisations, and line-managers are not expected to coach their direct reports, for fun. The coaching is expected to produce *results* – measurable returns – so let the ends define the means, let the outputs guide the inputs, let the required results from coaching inform the coaching approach. However, most organisations for which I have worked have a limited expectation of the results that effective coaching can deliver. So, my proposition is about what effective coaching can be.

Before I make a proposition for effective coaching, I need to introduce you to the core concept of The Inner Game. I realise I am in danger of being seen to contradict myself and define coaching by an approach. But the intent is not that. In order to make the proposition clear, I want you to see just what the scope of effective coaching can be and to understand a little more of what we, as human beings, are capable of. I don't mean this in some naive, idealistic sense. I am talking results.

THE INNER GAME

The Inner Game of Tennis is perhaps one of most influential books on performance and learning of the last thirty years. It caused a huge stir when it was published and the ideas in it have been embraced by many thousands of people all over the world. Clearly the ideas apply to many areas of life beyond the tennis court. It was written by Timothy Gallwey in 1974, is still in print and has been followed by other titles, not least *The Inner Game of Work*.

Let me introduce you to one of the core concepts. The way I have it starts with two words:

Potential   Performance

I have put these words on the page with a gap between them, because there is always a gap between performance and potential. And it is a huge gap. Even in the most ordinary activity, no matter how good someone is, they can always do better. However, there is something in the gap, and understanding what it is can help bridge it. I can remember occasions playing competitive tennis, becoming anxious and distracted. The little voice inside my head would start saying things like 'you can't let this loser win, what would they say in the changing room? Watch the ball. I hope he doesn't serve to my backhand. Just push it back into play, play safe. No, hit it cross court. You idiot ...' And so on.

Galway called thoughts like these 'interference'. Interference is usually based in fear and doubt. I would argue that nothing gets in the way of peak performance more than doubt. So the model becomes

Potential   minus   interference
is equal to   Performance

Thus one way to increase performance is to reduce the interference. As the interference gets less, more of the potential is available. Interference crops up in many forms. Here is a partial list that you might find familiar.

- Fear (of losing, of winning, of making a fool of yourself)
- Lack of self confidence
- Trying too hard
- Trying for perfection
- Trying to impress
- Anger and frustration
- Boredom
- A busy mind.

One of the ways to reduce interference is to focus attention. When the attention is focused the player enters a mental state in which he can learn and perform at his best. Gallwey called that mental state 'relaxed concentration'. Most people that I ask have had an experience of this mental state, also called 'flow'. For some it has been a profound and moving experience, very often when engaged in a physical activity. A friend of mine used to race motorbikes and, occasionally, when he was absolutely on the limit, with his attention glued to the rider in front of him, he would get into flow. His thoughts and actions would become one, time would seem to slow down and the noise of the engines appear to diminish. In this state he would sense exactly when the rider in front was going to make a tiny mistake and capitalise on it without hesitation. Being in flow does not have to be quite so dramatic. It can occur in such mundane activities as writing. You sit down at your desk and get started. You make a number of false starts; it is just not quite right. You get up, close the door, sit down and start again. And, suddenly, the words begin to come. You become engrossed in the task. You look at your watch, an hour has gone by and you did not even notice it. And the report is half written. From the perspective of The Inner Game a key part of the line-manager or coach's role is to help reduce the interference that affects the people he works with. This would be a remarkable shift of focus.

I will try to give some more life to this core concept by describing a demonstration that a colleague gave at a coaching skills workshop. It is an adaptation of an exercise that Gallwey uses and shows quite clearly what happens when the coach is truly committed to the player's learning and does not get in the way of that learning with instructions, advice or suggestions. Interestingly, this approach is not reliant on the coach being an expert in the topic of the session. In fact there is not one instruction or suggestion in the whole session; *the coach is working with the individual's capacity to learn.* My understanding is that wrapped up in an individual's 'potential' is this learning capacity. Learning is hard-wired. The topic for the session is 'how to improve catching', in this case catching a ball. It requires a willing volunteer from the group who believes that he cannot catch.

The coach positioned himself about twelve feet away from the volunteer and addressed him: 'To start with, let's just see if you can catch at all. OK?'. The volunteer, Peter, nodded but did not say anything. The coach threw a ball to him. Peter held out both his hands stiffly in front of him and his face screwed up with fear and anticipation. The ball passed just over the top of his hands, thumped into his chest and fell to the floor. Embarrassed, Peter grew even more tense.

The coach threw another ball. Peter reached out as before and missed completely. The coach threw another with the same result. 'Is that what you would expect?', the coach asked. 'Absolutely', Peter replied in a small voice. 'I told you I couldn't catch and never could. Teachers in school would put me in goal just to get a laugh.' 'Is that what you're thinking when I throw the ball?' 'That, and … and all these people watching.'

The coach looked around at the people, some of whom had stood up and now formed in a loose circle around them. 'Ah, don't worry about us' came a kindly voice.

The coach paused and caught Peter's attention again. 'Tell me,

Peter', he said, 'if your catching was to get better, how would we know?'

'Well, I'd catch them, wouldn't I?'

'All of them?'

'Some of them.'

'How many out of ten?'

'Would you throw them in exactly the same way as before?', Peter enquired suspiciously. The coach nodded. 'Then to catch one out of ten would be amazing.'

'I know. And what would give you a real sense of achievement?'

'I'll say three out of ten.'

'OK. Stay with me – I'm going to throw you some more balls. What I want you to do is watch the ball when it's in flight and, when you've caught it or whatever, tell me what you noticed about it. OK?'

'So I'm to tell you what I notice about the ball when it's flying towards me.'

'Exactly.'

The coach threw a ball. It brushed Peter's fingers as it went by him. 'What did you notice about the ball?'

'Nothing.'

'OK. Tell me what you notice about this one.' Again he threw a ball. Again Peter failed to catch. 'It's just yellow, greeny-yellow.'

Peter's response drew a snigger from the group. The coach, without taking his eyes from Peter, put a finger across his lips and the laughter stopped. 'Fine. Tell me what you notice this time.' He threw another.

'It's got some writing on it,' said Peter as the ball bounced out of the palm of his hand.

'Fine, so you notice the colour and the writing. Which is most interesting?'

'The writing.'

'OK. Tell me some more about the writing.' He threw a ball again.

'The writing is spinning, the ball is spinning', said Peter as he caught the ball. There was a sharp intake of breath from behind. The coach did not respond.

'Shall we stay with the spin?', he asked. Peter nodded. 'Tell me what you notice about the spin.' And once more the coach threw a ball.

'It's spinning towards me, quite fast', said Peter as he caught again.

'You noticed both the direction and the speed of the spin. Which is most interesting?' Peter paused. He threw the ball back to the coach. 'Er … the direction.'

'OK. Tell me which way this one is spinning', the coach asked, and then threw a ball. Peter reached out towards the ball and gracefully caught it, pulling his hands back towards himself in the act of catching, like a confident cricket player. He was completely relaxed, focused. 'The top is spinning towards me and a little to the side.'

'Which side?'

'This way', Peter said, and described the direction of his finger in the air.

'And this one?', the coach asked as he threw another.

'Spinning the other way.'

'And this one?' This one Peter completely failed to catch.

'What did you notice that time?'

'Nothing at all.'

'So where was your attention?' Peter's face creased into a big grin. 'I was thinking that I was catching for the first time in my life. Incredible!' He started laughing. The group clapped and laughed with him. 'How did you do that?'

'We'll come back to that. Tell me, how did you do in relation to our goal – to catch three out of ten?'

'I've no idea. I must have caught three, though.'

One of the other participants in the workshop observed: 'You caught five out of eight by my counting.'

'Wow. That many.'

'Peter, are you willing to stop the exercise?'

'Ah, just one more. No go on, it's fine.'

The coach turned to the participant who had made the observation. 'What did you notice about the exercise?' The participant thought for a second. 'Mostly that you didn't tell him how to catch. You gave him no technical instruction.' 'Anything else?', asked the coach. Someone else added in: 'What I noticed was how you made Peter concentrate.' 'How did I do that?'

There was a pause. 'You just asked him what he noticed …' 'Yes.' 'And then …'

Here Peter joined in. 'I noticed the colour and the writing … and you asked me to choose one … and I chose the writing.'

'Yes. And then?'

Nobody seemed to remember so the coach filled in the blank: 'I think I asked you to tell me what you noticed about the writing.'

'That's right, that's when I noticed that it was spinning', Peter answered.

'I see what you were doing', another participant said. 'Each time Peter looked at the ball he noticed something more, some more detail, so after a while he was concentrating completely.'

'Yes,' Peter added in, 'and the more I concentrated the less I noticed the other people and I kind of forgot that I couldn't catch.'

Another voice from the group asked: 'But how did he learn how to catch?'

'To a degree he already knew. Peter's seen others doing it and has tried before. So he had some information already. But, more importantly, with each attempt he learned something more, unconsciously. Peter always had the potential to learn how to catch. Notice I did not say that there was a great catcher within him just waiting to get out; this is about the potential to learn quickly and in a way that's fun. It's just that self-doubt and fear were getting in the way of the learning. When he got really focused the fear and doubt were forgotten and his natural ability to learn came to the fore. And I'll bet that if I had tried to teach in the more traditional way and given instructions, he would have got more tense and fearful and would have failed yet again.'

It is difficult to communicate on paper just how extraordinary the exercise described above is. Most people who witness it are completely taken by surprise. They have never seen such a dramatic shift in performance. They have never seen someone learn so quickly. They have seldom seen so much joy in so simple an exercise. Having seen the exercise, most people want to know what happened and what the coach did. The realisation that the coach did very little and that there was no technical instruction involved is the second surprise of the day. In a sense the paradigm that most people operate from, which tells them about how people learn and how quickly they can learn, has been blown apart. And that therefore the coach's primary responsibility is not to teach but to facilitate learning. For some this experience can be really uncomfortable and they will not believe the evidence of their eyes.

EFFECTIVE COACHING: THE PROPOSITION

I suggested earlier in this chapter that one way through the apparent confusion about coaching would be to let the ends define the means. So first I have to make a statement about those ends and then suggest how they might be achieved. And in so doing I am putting forward a proposition about what effective coaching *can* be.

Effective coaching in the workplace delivers achievement, fulfilment and joy from which both the individual and the organisation benefit. By achievement I mean the delivery of extraordinary results, organisational and individual goals achieved, strategies, projects and plans executed. It suggests effectiveness, creativity and innovation. Effective coaching delivers achievement, which is sustainable. Because of the emphasis on learning and because the confidence of the player is enhanced ('I worked it out for myself!') the increase in performance is typically sustained for a longer period and will impact on areas that were not directly the subject of the coaching.

In fulfilment I include learning and development. To achieve the business result is one thing, to achieve it in a way in which the player learns and develops as part of the process has a greater value – to the player, the line-manager or coach and the organisation, for it is the capacity to learn that ensures an organisation's survival. I also include here the notion that work can be meaningful; that individuals through coaching begin to identify goals that are intrinsically rewarding. With fulfilment comes an increase in motivation. That the coach respects the player, his ideas and opinions, that the player is doing his work in his own way, that he is pursuing his own goals and is responsible – all this makes for a player who is inspired and committed. In this way more of the energy, intelligence and imagination of each individual is brought to the service of the organisation.

And joy. When people are achieving their goals, when those goals have some meaning and when learning and developing is part of the process, enjoyment ensues. These three components, achievement, fulfilment and joy, are interlinked and the absence of any one will impact and erode the others. Learning without achievement quickly exhausts one's energy. Achievement without learning soon becomes boring. The absence of joy erodes the human spirit.

There is one other factor that I cannot fit neatly into the three outputs of effective coaching, but is implicitly behind them all, and this is responsibility. Without responsibility and a sense of ownership, organisations quickly become ineffective. Coaching directly and immediately impacts on responsibility. If the line-manager or coach solves the problem or decides on the course of action for the player then he has taken ownership and responsibility. Should the player hit an obstacle he will come back to the line-manager or coach for more guidance. Coaching in which the player defines his own goals, solves a problem for himself or develops his own plan, has the result that responsibility stays with the player.

These ends, achievement, fulfilment and joy, cannot be delivered through an approach to coaching in which the line-manager or coach instructs others as a function of their expertise, knowledge or, worse, status. This approach, as I will explain in greater depth in the next chapter, is known as 'directive'. A wholly directive approach reduces the opportunity for the player to think or be creative, limits the possibility of their taking responsibility and takes any satisfaction or joy out of what limited achievement there might be. Effective coaching, as described above, requires a predominantly 'non-directive' approach, an approach that evokes excellence, in which learning is intrinsic and satisfaction derives from the pursuit and achievement of meaningful goals. This is what effective coaching can be.

Chapter 3
Non-directive coaching

This chapter and the next, which describes my understanding of the inner game as it applies to coaching, contain the core notions of effective coaching. I was tempted to put the inner game chapter first to honour the chronology of their appearance, but felt that the non-directive models would present an easier entry point, a place from which you could easily get started and begin to put the ideas into practice. The non-directive 'school', as I know it, is essentially an offshoot of The Inner Game, although it has borrowed much from other sources, not least Carl Rogers. It was developed in the UK by some of the people mentioned in the acknowledgements at the front of the book and by myself. There are a number of models and techniques that are particular to it. My colleagues and I at The School of Coaching have subsequently worked with, developed and clarified these ideas and I present them here. In this chapter I will take you through a definition of coaching, make some distinctions around the notions of directive and non-directive coaching and describe in some detail a fundamental model (known as GROW).

A DEFINITION

The following is a definition of coaching that has some currency and that we use at The School of Coaching:

Coaching is the art of facilitating the performance, learning and development of another.

It is worth looking at some of the individual words in this definition. I will start with the word **performance**. Coaching in business is ultimately concerned with performance and anything a coach might say or do should be driven by the intention to improve performance. Improved performance may relate to the execution of a specific task or project, the achievement of business goals or more generically greater effectiveness or efficiency.

Learning is another potential outcome from coaching and is at least as important as performance because, taking a longer-term view, the future performance of the organisation depends on it. The distinction I would make from **development** is that while you have to learn in order to develop, learning as used here refers to a broad domain, how to approach a task, getting to grips with new technology, while development is about personal growth and greater self-awareness.

Then I come to **facilitating**. Here it means more than 'to make easy', although that is desirable too. Facilitating implies that the person being coached has the capacity to think something through for himself, to have an insight or creative idea. It acknowledges that people can learn without being taught. This in turn means that the coach has to give up on the fact that he has the right answer. The role of the coach is to enable the player to explore, to gain a better understanding, to become more aware and from that place to make a better decision than they would have made anyway.

Which leaves **art**. I do not mean to suggest that there is no science to coaching, for there is and it forms much of the content of this book. Coaching is an art in the sense that when practised with excellence, there is no attention on the technique: the coach is fully engaged with the player and the process of coaching becomes a dance between two people, conversationally moving in complete harmony and partnership. At this point the intelligence, intuition and imagination of the coach become a valuable contribution – rather than being interference for the player. The science to coaching comes out of experience and observations shared with like-minded people over a number of years and supported by other, related, disciplines such as psychology or philosophy. Much of this book is devoted to a description of that science, but you should know that the science of coaching is not coaching. If you get stuck in doing it by the book you are truly stuck, for your attention is with the book or the right way of doing it and not with the player. Someone once said of acting 'there are no rules but you've got to know them', and coaching is a bit like that.

THE SPECTRUM OF COACHING SKILLS

Coaching is a relationship and the conversation that takes place within that relationship can take a number of forms depending on the situation and the needs of the player. Diagram 1 lays out most of the different conversational approaches a coach might take during a coaching session.

The most important distinction made in the diagram is between directive and non-directive coaching. This builds on the observations I made in the previous section about facilitation. Directive means just that; to direct, to tell, to instruct. It is the form of education and management that we are most familiar with. It has its genesis in our earliest days and then all the way through our schooling. Teacher knows and, like it or not, will tell you. You, on the other hand, sit there passively. The assumption is that once you have been told you will know. And if you did not get it the first time around, the teacher merely has to increase the volume. (Because everyone knows that there is a direct correlation between understanding and volume.)

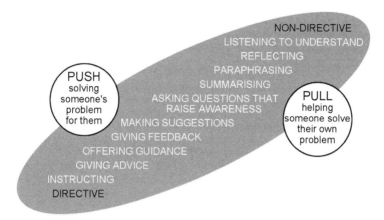

Diagram 1. The spectrum of coaching skills.

There is an in-built limitation in the directive approach, which is that the coach has to know the answer already, or has to be able to work it out. Given the structure in most organisations, where there are so many people with different specialisms and unique issues reporting to a line-manager, that is an unrealistic proposition. Surprisingly, the fact that we do not know the answer does not seem to stop some of us. Occasionally, as part of a training programme to develop coaching skills, I take the participants onto the tennis court. The purpose in this is to get them to deepen their non-directive coaching skills, the theory being that if they do not know the techniques involved in playing tennis they cannot resort to instructions. What baffles me is that participants who have never played tennis before will still try to tell their player how to play. It seems that the directive modelling of those early years is very powerful; people are trapped in 'teaching' and do not see that teaching has little to do with learning. What is amazing, and it amazes me every time I see it, is the results these coaches achieve when they adopt a non-directive approach. People learn in minutes things that would take a coach, operating from a more conventional model, hours to teach.

Non-directive coaching is, again, just that. You do not direct, instruct or tell. Let me remind you how you learned to walk. You learned to walk through direct experience, a kind of trial and error. You stood up and had a go. You fell over. Unconsciously your body–mind processed the information gained from that experience, took account of the results, and unconsciously made the appropriate corrections. Most of us walk reasonably well and few have had any direct instruction in how to do it. Let me also tell what did not happen when you learned to walk. A willing parent did not stand behind you, armed with 'The Book That Has Been Handed Down Through The Ages' and issue a series of instructions: 'Good boy. Now put all your weight on your right leg. OK. Let your left leg swing forward. Try to get some balance with your arms, no, stupid, your left leg …'. You get the picture. Nor were there recriminations, punishments and blame when you got it wrong. Parents in the early days are blessed with a non-judgemental approach that encourages experimentation and playfulness. And then somewhere along the way we, as parents, teachers and line-managers, forget this. As I have said, each one of us is born with an innate capacity to learn, a sort of learning instinct, if you will. A non-directive coach seeks to tap into that instinct so that the player learns for himself.

Despite my passionate insistence about the limitations of a directive or 'tell' approach, it is important to understand that the directive end of the spectrum is also available to you as a coach. There will be times when you *do* know the answer and the player is stuck. There will be times when your player needs some feedback or advice. In these situations, to withhold an answer, feedback or advice would not be helpful. However, the magic inhabits the non-directive end of the spectrum.

THE GROW MODEL

This next section details how to manage a coaching conversation. As will be obvious by now, you cannot manage the content of the conversation; that belongs to the player. However, to be effective when coaching you need to manage yourself and the structure and process of the session. The idea of managing yourself is addressed in Chapter 12, 'The art of coaching', and is a life-long journey. Being in control of the structure and the process is an easier game.

The GROW model (Diagram 2) enables the line-manager or coach to structure a coaching conversation and deliver a meaningful result. The practice of effective coaching was already in place before the GROW model was 'discovered'. The early practitioners

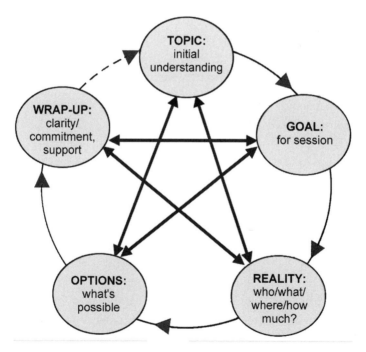

Diagram 2. The GROW model.

of coaching worked more or less intuitively. Over time it became apparent that in the more successful sessions there was a certain sequence of key stages. The pattern was discussed and formulated as the GROW model. The model grew out of best practice and not theory. I tell you this because for many people the first use of the model feels unnatural and you should know that once you have used it a few times it begins to feel fluent, to the point where you hardly have to think of it, or refer to it only as a sort of checking point if the conversation is not going well.

The first letters of each of the stages in the model give you GROW. Well, almost. What is missing is the first and rather critical stage, that of identifying the *topic* for the session. The attempts to include this stage in the mnemonic have, without exception, been clumsy – the best was the To Grow model, borrowing the 'To' from topic. In any case it was too late to change it because the model had already gained considerable currency.

If you imagine someone coming to you for some coaching, a sequence of questions that went something like

'What do you want to talk to me about?'	(Topic)
'What's actually happening?'	(Reality)
'What could you do about it?'	(Options)
'What are you definitely going to do about it?'	(Wrap-up)

would be an obvious and natural path to take. The only missing element from the perspective of the model is the goal. Let me take you through each of the stages of the model.

Topic

This is the first stage in any coaching conversation. It is not a detailed account of the subject matter at this point. What you want is to understand what territory you are in, the scale of the topic, the importance and sometimes the emotional significance for the player. It is sometimes useful to establish what the player's longer-term vision or goal for the topic is. At this stage the coach's intention is to understand what specifically the player wants to talk about.

COACH   What would you like to talk about?

PLAYER   As you know I've got to make a presentation to the Board next week and I'm a bit nervous about doing a good job.

COACH   Tell me some more about that.

PLAYER   The team have asked me to make the presentation on Project Blue and I am not at all sure how I should approach it.

COACH   Right.

PLAYER   And if I tell the truth I'm a bit nervous about standing up before the Board. They have a reputation for being tough on people who don't present well.

COACH   Yes, I know. Is there anything else about this?

PLAYER   Not really. Well, yes, the last time I made a presentation to a senior group it did not go very well.

COACH   Let me check. Is there a broader issue here about your presentation skills?

PLAYER   I guess so.

COACH   Specifically then, what is the topic for the session?

PLAYER   It's about making a good presentation to the Board, and also about improving my presentation skills in general.

COACH   If you could make progress with those skills, how would you want it to be?

Goal

While all the stages of the model are critical, the Goal stage has perhaps the greatest impact on the success of the coaching conversation. In fact, 'goal' is not the best word to describe this stage. The coach is trying to establish the desired *outcome* for the conversation, something that will be achieved within the confines of the discussion, not the longer-term objective that the player has. For example, a goal or vision to generate £400,000 of new sales in the next three months (which could not be achieved within the coaching conversation – unless it was a very long conversation) is different from an outcome, which might be to have a plan to deliver £400,000 of new sales in the next three months. I have an image of this for myself. I have a tent on a beach, rather Victorian with red and white stripes, like a Punch and Judy stall. Above the entrance is a sign that says, 'Your problems solved. $100 or your money back'. (That sum was $50 in the first edition of the book.) When my client enters we establish a contract in the form of an achievable outcome for the coaching. I do not get paid unless that outcome is delivered. This outcome is typically an action step, a plan, a new idea or simply to have thought some issue through. The tent, just so you know, is somewhere warmer than the UK, otherwise the season would not be long enough to make a decent living.

In the goal stage the coach's intention is to identify and agree a number of clear and achievable outcomes.

COACH   OK, I think I've got a fair understanding of the topic. Tell me what you would like to get out of this session.

PLAYER   Well, I'm more concerned about the immediate problem, the presentation to the Board, than I am about reaching the longer-term thing – being happy to speak to groups of 50 or more. So I'd like to focus more on that.

COACH   Fine. And tell me what you want from this session.

PLAYER   Well, I'd like to understand what went wrong in the presentation to the senior managers that I mentioned and then to have an idea of the key things to do differently next week.

COACH   There are two bits in that. To understand what went wrong and to have an idea of the key things to do differently. Take the first bit. What outcome would you want from understanding what went wrong?

PLAYER   To have identified the key lessons.

COACH   What does key mean?

PLAYER   The most important. The two or three things that make or break a presentation.

COACH   And for the second bit? The key things to do differently. What outcome would you like from that?

PLAYER   Obviously the discussion about what went wrong may give me some of the things to do differently but I suspect there are some other things that I need to know.

COACH   And the outcome?

PLAYER   If I could find in the whole session five or six key things to do or remember, that would be great.

COACH   So let me summarise where we've got to …

Reality

This stage of the model is concerned with achieving the most accurate picture of the topic possible. The coach encourages the player to discuss and become more aware of all aspects of the topic. In this phase the primary function of the coach is to understand: not to solve, fix, heal, make better or be wise, but to understand. No analysis, no problem solving, no wisdom, no good ideas, no jumping to conclusions. The magic is that it is in that moment of understanding that the player understands for themselves, becomes more aware and is then in a position to make better decisions and choices than they would have done anyway.

In this stage the coach's intention is to create the clearest possible understanding of the topic.

COACH   You've mentioned the presentation that didn't work so well and then this other, more generic 'other things you might do'. Are there any other elements to this?

PLAYER   Not that I can think of.

COACH   Which of the two do you want to tackle first?

PLAYER   I think the obvious place to start is with the presentation that I messed up.

COACH   OK. Tell me about that.

PLAYER   It was in an earlier stage of this project and again it was my turn to present – we take it in turns. I thought it was going to be relatively straightforward but in the event it turned out all wrong.

COACH   Just how bad was it?

PLAYER   It wasn't a complete disaster and they did get the message. It was that I really didn't do the work we had done, or myself, justice.

COACH   So what actually happened?

PLAYER   I was a bit flustered when I got there. We had worked late the night before and at that point I thought I knew what I had to do. However, on the morning I felt unprepared. I was still putting the slides in order minutes before I was due to start.

COACH   What else happened?

PLAYER   Apart from not feeling prepared I was really nervous and my words came out a bit scrambled. At one point someone asked me to repeat what I had just said because they had not understood.

COACH   Was there anything else in the session that did not work for you?

PLAYER   Yes. I was put out by a number of the questions. I don't think that anyone was trying to be difficult, I just found it difficult to find the answers.

COACH   So far in this conversation you've mentioned something about your preparation, about feeling nervous, and the difficulty you had in answering questions. Is there anything else that you remember?

PLAYER   Not really. That's enough to work with.

COACH   Which of those three things would you like to focus on first?

PLAYER   The bit about handling questions. That was the worst bit.

Options

Once the clearest possible understanding of the situation or topic has been reached, the discussion naturally turns to what can be done, to what it is possible for the player to do. I use 'possible' as in 'that's a possibility', in the biggest, most creative sense, rather then in a narrow, restrictive one. In the reality phase a clear understanding is gained and it is from this understanding that the possibilities emerge. The intention here is to draw out a list of all that is possible without judgement or evaluation.

COACH   We've spoken about preparation, nervousness, and handling questions in some depth now. In looking to move forward, which of those would you like to pursue first?

PLAYER   I still think there is most mileage in the 'handling questions' bit. If I can get that right it will help with the nervousness issue and the preparation bit should be easy to crack.

COACH   Where we got to with handling questions, as I understood you, was that you felt that you had not always fully understood the question.

PLAYER   Yes, and that was partly because I was thinking of my next slide.

COACH   So what could you do differently?

PLAYER   I could make sure that no questions were asked till the end of the session.

COACH   What else?

PLAYER   I could just stop myself from going to the next slide – maybe make eye contact. That would help.

COACH   Anything else?

PLAYER   Not sure. Well, if I haven't heard I could ask the questioner to repeat the question, or if I think I've heard but I'm not sure, I suppose I could check my understanding by repeating the question.

COACH   What else can you think of?

Wrap-up

The final stage of the model, with lots of options on the table. What remains is to select the most appropriate and agree the next steps. It is often useful to check the player's commitment to the chosen course of action and to see if any support is required. It is almost always useful to get the player to say exactly what their action plan is – some coaches have a tendency to say, 'so your action plan is …'. If the player states the action plan it ensures clarity and agreement and, from the tone of voice, the coach can ascertain the level of commitment. In this stage the coach's intention is to gain commitment to action.

COACH   Of all the options that we have identified which ones do you think you might action?

PLAYER   I can't remember them all.

COACH   I think I jotted down most of them. There are those options that came out of the discussion about the presentation, concerning preparation, nervousness and handling questions. Then there were the options that came out of the second part of the discussion. Where do you want to start?

PLAYER   Let's start with the handling questions bit.

COACH   You came up with four options: keeping the questions to the end of the session, stopping and making eye contact, asking the questioner to repeat the question and playing your understanding of the question back.

PLAYER   That's right. The only one I'm uncomfortable about is the first one; keeping questions till the end.

COACH   What is it that makes you uncomfortable?

PLAYER   Despite the fact that I am not very good at it – yet – I do want to keep the sessions as interactive as possible. So I think I'll skip that one. The others I can do.

COACH   Just so we are both sure, tell me specifically what you are going to do?

PLAYER   In the presentation to the Board when I hear a question I will stop thinking of what I have to do next and make eye contact with the questioner. If I don't hear the question fully I will either ask the person to repeat it, or, if I've got the gist of it I will check my understanding by playing it back.

COACH   OK. Now which part do you want to tackle next?

The GROW model: summary

Let me see if I can make this even clearer with an analogy. It is not entirely watertight but works very well in as far as it goes. When the player begins to talk it is most likely that their thoughts about the topic are unclear and jumbled up. It's a bit like a jigsaw puzzle, only in this case the pieces are in a bag and there is no cover picture to act as a guide. As the player talks, the corner pieces and some of the edges are identified and put on the table. The scale and the nature of the topic thus become a little clearer. At this point it is possible to set a goal (outcome), as both the coach and the player broadly know what they are discussing. Moving to the reality phase, the player is encouraged to put all the pieces of the jigsaw, or almost all, on the table. And as the conversation progresses the player will notice that some of the pieces are face down and others in the wrong place. As most of the pieces are turned face-up and shuffled into the right place the picture or pattern emerges. The player sees the whole picture, has a new insight or comes to a solution or a possible option. From this point the player can typically begin to make some choices about the next steps.

The GROW model is shown in Diagram 2 as a circle because in the most straightforward sessions you move from topic to goal to reality to options to wrap-up and then maybe contract to a time and a place for the next conversation. The arrows between the stages reflect the fact that not all sessions are straightforward and that you may have to shuffle between the stages. For instance, in the wrap-up stage the player may identify a new option, or in the reality stage it may become clear that the goal is not appropriate. If this happens, simply return to the relevant part of the model. Do not get stuck in its linear nature – few players think in a strictly linear fashion and your job is to follow their interest.

THE MODEL T

You will have begun to gather that the role of the coach is to encourage the player to think, and not to think for them. The need is to stay on their agenda and to follow their interest. This is not an easy thing to do at first because most of your instincts will be to think about the issue and to try to solve it. What I have noticed over a number of years is that when I suggest that this instinctive response will not help the player, many coaches in training are at a loss as to know what to do instead. This is where the Model T comes in, so known because of the way it is presented diagrammatically (Diagram 3).

The Model T is a remarkably powerful technique for making progress in the GROW model. It suggests that you expand the con-

Diagram 3. The 'Model T'.

versation first, then focus on the detail. Imagine that you are in the options stage of the model. The conversation would go like this:

COACH   You've given me one option, to delegate the project to Jamie. What other options are there? [Expanding]

PLAYER   I could give it to Jamie but still supervise it myself.

COACH   Anything else? [Expanding again]

PLAYER   I could do it myself.

COACH   Anything else?

PLAYER   I can't think of anything.

COACH   OK. But let's see if there are any other options. Tell me what you would really like to do, regardless of consequences. [Expanding again and adding a little creativity]

PLAYER   Well, what I'd really like is not to do it at all. But … that's not realistic. But … having said that I could delay it for a couple of weeks till I'm less busy.

COACH   So, four options then. Hand it to Jamie completely, hand it to Jamie and you supervise, do it yourself and delay it till later. Which of those is most interesting? [Focusing and leaving choice and responsibility with the player]

The Model T has some inherent benefits. Often in coaching the temptation is to seek resolution as quickly as possible. There are many dangers in this, not least that the coach starts driving the agenda. A second danger is that, in the attempt to make progress, information that might be relevant is omitted. The Model T keeps the coach on the player's agenda, and because it suggest that you expand the conversation before going into detail most, if not all, of the relevant information is picked up in the conversation.

The model can also be used in the topic or reality phases. If a player describes a particular aspect of an issue and the coach says 'tell me some more about that' (focusing), there is the possibility that time will be invested in discussing something that is not entirely relevant to the overall issue. Far better to ask 'is there anything else?' (expanding) and having heard any other aspects of the issue to focus on the aspect that appears to be most relevant.

COACH   So, you've told me that the project is behind and that you're going to miss the next milestone and you've also mentioned the poor performance of your team. Is there anything else? [Summarising, then expanding]

PLAYER   We have an internal client, a sponsor from the Board, who is also slowing things down.

COACH   The project, the team and the sponsor. Which is most interesting to discuss first? [Focusing]

PLAYER   Actually we should really talk about the sponsor. When we started the conversation I thought it was really all about the poor performance of the team, but without a clear remit from our sponsor it is always going to be difficult to be successful.

In this snippet of a coaching conversation you can see that if the coach had not 'expanded', a really important element of the issue might have been overlooked. The coach also used the word 'interesting' in the focusing question. Initially this surprises people; they are expecting words like 'relevant' or 'important'. If the coach had used the word 'important' instead, there is a possibility that it might have generated interference. For instance, the player might well become less relaxed as he tries to make the 'right' choice in a matter that the coach had indicated was 'important'. Far better to follow interest. Interest allows room for intuition and feelings amongst other things and will almost always generate a richer conversation.

POSTSCRIPT

I intended in this chapter to present some of the most pragmatic tools available to the coach to enable you to get started. Before we move on to the next chapter, which gives further detail about The Inner Game, there are two things I should point out. The first is that, although the non-directive school derives from The Inner Game in great part, I have never heard Tim Gallwey use the term 'non-directive'. I remember an occasion where he took over a demonstration that a colleague was giving – the ball-catching exercise described in Chapter 2 – and implicitly changed the goal by throwing the ball with great speed and getting the guinea pig in the demonstration to catch with their non-dominant hand. After the exercise my colleague questioned him on this. His response? 'I just believed in her capacity to learn.' The truth is of course that it is impossible to be completely non-directive and probably not entirely desirable. A slight raising of the eyebrow, a change in the breathing pattern, these are all subtle signs that may give away your thoughts or feelings that the player may well pick up on. To get an insight into how to manage this quandary you may want to check out Chapter 12. But for now, the next chapter. Let me introduce you to some of the key ideas in The Inner Game.

Chapter 4
Effective coaching and The Inner Game

It's cold. It's a wet and somewhat windy autumnal day in the south of England. And it's early. I am at a golf driving range waiting for Patrick, the CEO of a large engineering company, who is interested in finding out about my approach to coaching and the influence of The Inner Game. He arrives and I discover that he has his HR Director with him. He introduces me as he takes his clubs from the car and we make our way to the end bay in the range. I get him to loosen up by hitting a few balls. He plays golf about ten times a year, mostly for business reasons, and has had a few golf lessons.

'Which part of your game are you most interested in improving?'

Patrick looks at the clubs in his bag, hesitates and then says: 'My driving. I don't seem to be able to get the length that others do. And I tend to slice it.'

I put a ball on the tee in front of him. 'Show me.'

Patrick hits the ball. Sure enough it begins to turn to the right and just about reaches the 150 yard marker. He hits another ball and the result is much the same. 'Is that what you'd expect?' He nods his head. 'Yes. I am not very coordinated and have always avoided sports of any kind. I only play because some of my clients like to do business on the golf course. And it's worse with clients because they're all watching you perform.'

'Right. If we were to be really successful here what kind of shot would you be hitting at the end of the session?'

'I guess the ball would bounce just beyond the 175 yard marker and would be fairly straight.'

'How would we know that it was straight?'

'It would be between those trees to the right on the horizon and the electricity pylon. In that "corridor".'

'OK. Here's what I want you to do. First, don't worry about the goal for the moment. Forget about it in fact. We'll come back to it later. Now, I want you to hit a few balls and simply tell me what you notice.'

'How do you mean?'

'Try this. Stand on one foot and put all your attention into the foot on the ground. Exactly. What do you notice?'

'It's balancing.'

'That is not what you notice – that is what you think about what you notice, a concept. There's a world of difference. Tell me what you actually notice.'

'It's wobbling.'

'Be more precise.'

'The foot is moving from side to side.'

'Is there anything else you notice?'

'I can feel my weight over the front of my foot, over the ball.'

'Now what I want you to do is to hit a golf ball and to simply notice what you are doing.'

Patrick hits a few balls. 'I am noticing my hips moving, coming through too early.'

'Too early?'

'That's what the pro tells me.'

'Fine, but don't worry about that for the moment. Hit a few more and tell me what you notice this time.'

'I noticed that I did not make good contact on the last two and, there's something else, the stroke feels a bit funny.'

'Funny?'

'Yes, more … it's kind of jerky.'

'You've noticed three things: your hips, the contact between the ball and the club and this jerky business. Hit some more and tell me which is the most interesting. What stands out?'

'The jerkiness.'

'Hit a few more and don't try to change anything. Tell me where exactly in the stroke it feels jerky.'

Patrick hits some more.

'It's in the downswing.'

'All through the downswing or just a bit of it?'

He hits another ball. 'It's in the second half of the downswing.'

'Great. Hit another and tell me where it is this time.'

'Interesting. That one was just in the last quarter.'

'Hit another.'

'Amazing.'

'What is?'

'There's no jerkiness there.'

'If there's no jerkiness what do you notice in its place?'

Patrick hits some more. He's smiling now. 'Fluidity.'

'Tell me after the next stroke how fluid it was. Use a scale of one to ten.'

He hits a ball. 'About 5.' Another ball. 'Hmm. More.'

'Where's more on a scale of one to ten?'

'Six. Maybe seven.'

Another ball. 'Seven.' Another. 'Eight.'

The HR Director has started laughing. Patrick looks up, mild surprise showing on his face. If he had not been so engrossed in noticing the fluidity quotient of his stroke he would have noticed that the ball was consistently flying straight and well past the 175 yard marker.

The lesson with Patrick is typical of many golf lessons I have given. If you go back through the script you will notice that I have not given one technical instruction. There are two reasons for this: one is that, as I have already explained, most instruction does not help people learn, and the second is that I don't play golf and therefore could not give a technical instruction even if I wanted to. But the golf coaching that I give is pretty successful. I am drawing your attention to this again because I really want you to appreciate that the coach's primary job is to help the player learn, not to teach. And you do not have to know very much about the discipline or topic in order to help someone learn. Remember, it's hard-wired.

I want to remind you that the concepts described in this chapter are my interpretation of The Inner Game. Imagine my shock and nervousness when I was delivering a session at a conference in Amsterdam and Tim Gallwey silently took a seat at the back (we had met for the first time the evening before). I was concerned that what I was presenting was congruent with his ideas. In writing this chapter I am experiencing a similar thing. So let me be clear about my intentions. There are elements of The Inner Game that I have 'made my own' and that fit particularly well with the notions of effective coaching. In this chapter I want to present my understanding of the principles and some of the most relevant techniques. Obviously the fundamental principles, the core philosophy of The Inner Game if you like, does more than just fit: it is the cornerstone of my approach. These are pure Gallwey.

The first lesson or distinction that we are offered is in the name, The Inner Game. Inner implies Outer. If you have ever had conventional golf tuition you will hear three things from the pro at the end: 'That will be $50 please', 'keep practising' and 'it's all in the mind'. The sequence of the statements is very important (to the pro). He knows he must ask for and get the money before making the last statement because, given that 'it is all in the mind' and the pro has done nothing to address the mind, no self-respecting client would pay up. However, I do not mean to malign golf pros. Most conventional tuition addresses the outer game – the techniques, the grips, the stance, the physical movement. And this is understandable as it is both visible and measurable. The contents of The Inner Game, on the other hand, are more elusive and cannot be observed or measured. These are things like perception, aspirations, values, fears and doubts. The models and techniques presented here offer an approach to addressing the inner game.

In the second chapter I introduced one of the key models in The Inner Game (potential minus interference is equal to performance) and suggested that the role of the coach is to reduce the interference, thus releasing more of the potential of the player. Patrick in the opening golf lesson exhibited a few fine examples of the type of interference I mean:

'Yes. I am not very coordinated and have always avoided sports of any kind. I only play because some of my clients like to do business on the golf course. And it's worse with clients because they're all watching you perform.'

Fear and doubt. Nothing interferes with human performance more. Fear and doubt fuel the outer game as we try to find the 'right' way to swing the club or deliver a presentation and thus create a self-perpetuating loop. Out of the fear that we may get it wrong we try to identify the 'right way', the right approach or technique. We then try to execute this 'right way' and this in turn becomes an interference, engendering more fear and doubt. Ivan Lendl, the tennis player, had numerous coaches (most of whom got fired) who tried to teach him their own unique right way to hit a forehand. He ultimately found his way, which was somewhat unconventional for the time, and, as is said, the rest is history.

The following anecdote is a slight diversion but is indicative of how invasive and constricting fear and doubt can be. I attended an event recently where a half a dozen or so 'captains of industry' were present. One of them started talking about the need for creativity in his organisation. A number of the others had a similar need. Within two minutes the conversation had turned to risk management. The message that they were communicating to the staff was something like 'I want more creativity but don't make a mistake'. And they were wondering why there was so little creativity in their organisation!

So interference is the prime obstacle to performance. On a Sunday night many years ago, when my stepdaughter Victoria was about eleven years old and on her way to bed, I asked whether all her homework had been completed. Her face fell; there was an English essay outstanding and she had to do it that night. Having just sat down to finish off the bottle of wine, I was not entirely delighted when my offer of help was accepted. We sat down side by side at the kitchen table. I asked what the topic of the essay was and wrote it down at the top of the page. I then asked what her thoughts were about the topic. Victoria knew the game well enough by this stage and knew that I was not going to write the essay but rather help her marshal her thoughts and get started. Knowing her to be very bright and full of ideas I was a little surprised and, yes, agitated when I got no answer. I turned to her with the intent of asking the question again – with more energy – when I noticed that she had curled up in the chair with her feet under her in a manner that still causes me to wonder at the flexibility of the human body. If her face had fallen earlier it had clearly not gone all the way and this time it was white as well. My agitation disappeared.

'What's up?'

'The essay should have been in on Friday and it's the third time that I have been late and Miss White is the only teacher who believes in me and now I've let her down and, and …'

'I see. What can you do about it?'

'Nothing.'

'Nothing?'

After a little while we got to 'If I finished the essay and got it to her first thing in the morning, and said sorry, maybe she won't be so cross with me and I would not have to sit through the whole morning worrying about the English class in the afternoon.'

'OK. Are you ready to do the essay?'

'Yes.'

'Tell me, what thoughts do you have about this topic?'

There followed a torrent of ideas. I jotted them down and read them back to her. Could she see a structure, a storyline? Yes. What more help did she need? I was to go away and let her finish. There was still an inch of wine.

THE TWO SELVES

When a person is focused and the interference, or most of it, is removed they enter into a different mental state sometimes called flow. Gallwey had a particular cut at this which he describes in *The Inner Game of Tennis*, which is very valuable. He noticed the capacity of people to have a conversation with themselves, and you can hear such conversations everyday, everywhere. Perhaps they are most evident in the sporting arena. These conversations are notable for the criticism, judgement and condemnation that individuals heap on themselves. There then typically follows a set of instructions about how to do whatever the task is better: 'You idiot, you know you should hit the ball in front of you. You're so lazy! Stay on your toes and get the racket back early ...'.

Gallwey asked, 'who is talking to whom?' and answers his own question thus: 'Obviously the who and the whom are separate entities or there would be no conversation, so that one could say that within each player there are two 'selves'. One ... seems to give instructions; the other ... seems to perform the action. Let's call the "teller" Self One and the "doer" Self Two.'

We describe Self One and Self Two at The School of Coaching as follows.

- Self One is the internalised voice of our parents, teachers and those in authority. Self One seeks to control Self Two and does not trust it. Self One is characterised by tension, fear, doubt and trying too hard.
- Self Two is the whole human being with all its potential and capacities including the 'hard-wired' capacity to learn. It is characterised by relaxed concentration, enjoyment and trust.

On workshops I will often ask people to describe moments when they have experienced Self Two. The first people to speak are usually those who engage in sport – skiing is a big one – followed by those who play music or sing. Then come the writers and the artists until everyone in the room can identify a time when they have 'been in flow'. As the conversation progresses, more and more situations are identified, including those that take place at work; writing a difficult report, a presentation, a sales meeting. In any moment, in any situation, you have the opportunity to be in either Self One or Self Two.

This has relevance here for three reasons.

- As a coach the aim is to operate from Self Two. This is where you will do your best and most rewarding work. I will talk about this in Chapter 10.
- When you coach another the aim is to help the player get into and stay in Self Two. In this way he can be the most objective, insightful, intuitive and creative.
- Helping the player to be in Self Two in everyday life and particularly in the critical moments such as key meetings and presentations is arguably part of the coach's or line-manager's role.

FOLLOWING INTEREST

There is no guaranteed method of getting into Self Two that I know of. However, I believe there is a key in what Gallwey called 'relaxed

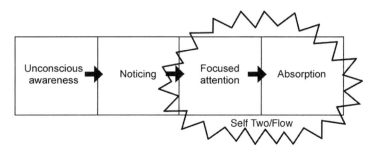

Diagram 4. The continuum of attention.

concentration'. This mental state, where the player is focused, relaxed and trusting, is another way of describing Self Two.

Let me suggest that there is a kind of continuum of attention (Diagram 4). It starts with what I call unconscious awareness where things are happening but you are not paying attention to them. As we move across the continuum we get to noticing; this is where you become conscious of what is in your attention, either as a function of choice or because it is compelling. Then there is focused attention and finally absorption where there is nothing else in your attention but the focus or the activity. On the right-hand side of the continuum you will tend to be in Self Two or Flow, the state in which you will perform and/or learn most effectively and enjoyably.

One approach that a coach might use to help a player move across the continuum I call following interest. Let me take a snippet from the golf lesson described earlier. Patrick's response below follows a question which was 'What do you notice?'.

'I am noticing my hips moving, coming through too early.'

'Too early?'

'That's what the pro tells me.' [Possibility for interference; judgement]

'Fine, but don't worry about that for the moment.' [Removing interference] 'Hit a few more and tell me what you notice this time.'

'I noticed that I did not make good contact on the last two and, there's something else, the stroke feels a bit funny.'

'Funny?'

'Yes, more … its kind of jerky.'

'You've noticed three things: your hips, the contact between the ball and the club and this jerky business. Hit some more and tell me which is the most interesting. What stands out?' [focusing by following interest; the Model T; see below]

'The jerkiness.'

'Hit a few more and don't try to change anything.' [Avoiding possible interference; trying to get it right] 'Tell me where exactly in the stroke it feels jerky.' [focusing attention]

Patrick hits some more. 'It's in the downswing.'

'All through the downswing or just a bit of it?'

He hits another ball. 'It's in the second half of the downswing.'

'Great. Hit another and tell me where it is this time.'

'Interesting. That one was just in the last quarter.'

'Hit another.'

'Amazing.' [Self Two/absorption; there is no judgement in 'amazing' just pleasure and awe]

'What is?'

'There's no jerkiness there.'

'If there's no jerkiness what do you notice in its place?'

Patrick hits some more. He's smiling now. 'Fluidity.'

'Tell me after the next stroke how fluid it was. Use a scale of one to ten.'

He hits a ball. 'About 5.' Another ball. 'Hmm. More.'

The process of following interest has this basic process at heart:

- Tell me what you notice.
- Tell me what else you notice.
- Of all the things you have noticed, which is most interesting?
- Tell me some more about that which is most interesting.

These ideas then allow me to develop the Model T, from the previous chapter, a little more. The horizontal bar of the T – Expand – is driven by noticing questions, and the vertical bar – Focus – is driven by interest.

'AWARENESS IS CURATIVE'

At the same time that the coach is following the interest of the player, something else is happening. The player is becoming more aware of what actually is happening, and as long as he does not try to analyse the data but simply notices and focuses on it then the natural process of learning will kick in. The title of this section is a quote from *The Inner Game of Work* and is, for many, almost counter-intuitive. I saw Gallwey work briefly with a woman some years back. She was a senior management consultant in what was one of the Big Five accountancy practices and had a problem with anxiety when faced with very senior clients such as CEOs. The conversation went something like this.

TIM   How anxious do you get, say on a scale of 1 to 10?

WOMAN   About 7 or 8.

TIM   Will you be meeting anyone with whom you might get anxious in the next few weeks?

The woman identified two or three such meetings.

TIM   What I suggest is that you rate your anxiety on a scale of 1 to 10 just before, during and after the meetings.

End of conversation. Awareness is curative.

A key part of becoming aware is the act, or is it the art, of noticing. Noticing is without judgement and is untainted by fear, doubt, aspiration or wish. Noticing is the 'not trying' of thinking. It allows in a much broader band and quantity of data and, as there is no judgement, eliminates interference. As I see it, this data is processed by Self Two and produces results effortlessly and elegantly that are often surprising.

THE PLAYER IN SELF TWO

In a coaching conversation one of the roles of the coach, as suggested earlier, is to help the player move into Self Two. This can be achieved through the process of following interest and becoming focused. The coach should also be observing the player with a little detachment, noticing the body language. It is useful for the coach to ask themself the question 'is the player in Self Two?'. If the answer is 'no', then a simple observation such as 'you look a little uncomfortable' can unlock the conversation. If a coaching conversation is stuck, look for the interference. There will be one – and it might be you. I recollect a coaching conversation with a partner in a large, international consultancy, who had some understanding of The Inner Game. We were discussing his career vision and goals and I confess I was falling off my chair with boredom. But this was a highly intelligent and creative man. So I asked him whether he was in Self One or Self Two:

D   Self One, I guess.

MYLES   What would it take for you to get into Self Two?

D   I'd have to stand up.

The answer surprised me a little.

MYLES   And what do I have to do?

D   You have to stand up too.

We started again, both of us walking around the room and, as you might imagine, the results were more exciting and challenging and more congruent with whom D actually was.

I hope it is clear that all of the techniques and models presented here can be used alongside or within the GROW model. Although what I am about to say next about the application of both approaches is not universally true, it holds good most of the time. In coaching you can have conversations about events and activities that are either *on-line* or *off-line*. On-line situations, that I might also call on-court, are situations where the player is considering how they will perform, how they will be in an activity. The conversation is focused in the actual moment of performing. Examples might include managing pressure in closing a sale or delivering a presentation. Off-line or off-court situations are those that are focused before or after the actual activity. Examples are thinking through an issue, planning for a future activity, or reviewing a past activity. Imagine the following coaching situation. A player is concerned about giving a particular presentation say in a couple of weeks' time. As the coaching progresses it emerges that there are two issues: one, she is not sure how to prepare for the event; and two, she is concerned that her nervousness while presenting will detract from the impact of the presentation. The first issue lends itself to a fairly straightforward GROW approach, while the second lends itself to an inner game approach. GROW is most useful in off-line situations where the player is planning something for the future, reviewing a past event, learning or solving a problem. The inner game is most useful in 'on-line' situations where a player is considering performance issues such as making a presentation or a sales visit.

I will often tell people with whom I am working about my understanding of these key Inner Game concepts because they become valuable tools for them to give their best performance in everyday life. For instance, I know that one of the quickest ways to get into Self Two is through enjoyment. Let me give you an example of how this works. In my youth I was a good tennis player and then latterly injury stopped me from playing. Eventually I had surgery to a damaged shoulder that sorted the problem. It was just after the rehabilitation process that I first hit some tennis balls. I had not played for years and was unfit but even so was surprised to find myself playing quite so badly. So, as a good apprentice in The Inner Game I tried a drill to focus attention and get into Self Two. Boy, I tried! After a while I was still playing appallingly and observed to myself that I was not enjoying it. Then it hit me – there must be some enjoyment in playing the game I love to play and in realising that the surgery had been a success. I rated my enjoyment on a scale of 1 to 10 as a 3. I played another rally and rated myself again. Still 3. Another rally and the rating this time was 5. And then 7's and 8's. As the enjoyment went up so did the quality of my tennis. What is interesting in this is that you cannot make yourself enjoy something; awareness is curative and, in this case, it transformed my performance. Now when working with colleagues at the School of Coaching on the programmes we run I will frequently ask, 'what is your level of enjoyment?' and then notice a slightly anxious face relax into a smile.

FLOW

I want to include some material here that does not come from The Inner Game school but which, as you will see, serves to support those ideas while adding greatly to the overall understanding. This material comes from Mihaly Csikszentmihalyi, Professor of Psychology at the University of Chicago. I compare the the state that Gallwey called Self Two with what Csikszentmihalyi calls 'Flow'. His most well-known book is *Flow, the Psychology of Happiness*. He describes flow as follows: 'In the flow state action follows upon action according to an internal logic that seems to need no conscious intervention by the actor.'

Daniel Goleman, in his book *Emotional Intelligence*, also refers to flow. I quote again: 'Flow is a state of self-forgetfulness, the opposite of rumination and worry. People in flow exhibit a masterly control of what they are doing, their responses perfectly attuned to the changing demands of the task.' A further quote from Goleman is: 'People perform at their best in flow ... the sheer pleasure of the act itself is what motivates them.'

Csikszentmihalyi (pronounced 'chick-sent-me-high-ee', I am told) describes the conditions that pertain in the flow experience. They include:

- There are clear goals every step of the way.
- There is immediate feedback to one's actions.
- There is a balance between the challenges and the skills required.
- Action and awareness are merged.
- Distractions are excluded from consciousness.
- There is no worry of failure.
- Self-consciousness disappears.
- The activity becomes autotelic (from the Greek; *auto* means self, *telos* means goal, so this means that the activity itself is its own reward).

If you read these conditions you will be able to see clearly the idea of interference expressed in a different form. For instance, the absence of a clear goal and feedback creates immense interference. On their own they are a wonderful checklist by which you might organise your work life, and that of those you coach.

POSTSCRIPT

In this chapter and the last I have tried to communicate the fundamental principles and models of effective coaching and above all to demonstrate the extraordinary capacity of human beings to learn and be creative. Human beings also have an extraordinary capacity to get in their own way and create interference for themselves. Let me give a final anecdote in this chapter. I was coaching the Operations Director of a medium-sized business who was trying to bring two parts of the business together into one unit.

BILL   The problem is that I can only see one way of doing it – and it's not very good.

[He described this 'one way'. He was right; it was not very good.]

MYLES   Tell me how else you could do it.

BILL   I told you I'm not very creative.

MYLES   I know, but if you were creative what would you come up with?

Bill looked at me and then laughed. The atmosphere changed and it was clear that I was not going to let him off the hook. It took another couple of minutes to identify three more options. Not creative? Nonsense.

The last word in this chapter should I think belong to Gallwey. I quote from his latest book *The Inner Game of Work*. I want to draw your attention to two words that he uses in this quote. The first is 'mobility'. Not movement; mobility – the capacity to move. What I read into this is that the choice to move rests with the player. The other word is 'caring': I do not need to explain that. '(Coaching) … must be learned mostly from experience. In the Inner Game approach coaching can be defined as the facilitation of mobility. It is the art of creating an environment, through conversation and a way of being, that facilitates the process by which a person can move towards desired goals in a fulfilling manner. It requires one essential ingredient that cannot be taught; caring not only for the external result but for the person being coached.'

Chapter 5
An introduction to the skills of effective coaching

This short chapter is an introduction to the skills of effective coaching and the purpose in writing it is twofold. Firstly, I want to bring together in one place all the skills that go to make up an effective coach so that the breadth and depth of the task of learning to coach can be appreciated. Secondly, I want to introduce a 'tool', the notion of intent, that defines the use and application of each of the skills.

The chart in Diagram 5 shows many and varied skills. The inclusion of some of the skills is obvious, such as listening and asking questions, while the presence of some others, such as hypothesising, is less so. The chart is an attempt to bring together all the skills that make a coach effective and as a consequence includes skills that are not necessarily deployed within the coaching conversation. I know that some part of the value that I add in coaching comes from the thinking that I do when I am walking the dog or because I have taken time to interview the people with whom the person I am coaching works and therefore have a good understanding of their organisational context; the key people, the culture, the strategy, etc.

In the chart I have grouped the various skills into skill sets, these sets being defined by a common intent. The skill sets are shown in the left-hand column of the chart. I then show the outward manifestation, the specific skill, in the right-hand column. Some skills show up in more than one set. The middle column describes the intent. Some of these skill sets merit a chapter of their own while

Skill sets	Intent	Specific skills
Generating understanding/ raising awareness	To help the player understand themself/ their situation more fully so that they can make better decisions	Listening in order to understand Repetition, paraphrasing and summarising Using silence Asking questions that follow interest Asking questions to clarify Grouping
Proposing	To make available to the player the coach's observations, knowledge, experience, intelligence, insight, intuition and wisdom	Giving feedback Making suggestions Giving advice Challenging Evoking creativity and innovation Giving instruction
Managing self	To ensure that the impact of the coach's needs and preconceptions on the player are minimised To maximise one's own performance as coach	Self awareness Boundary awareness Transparency Clarifying intent Entering 'flow'/Self Two
Structuring	To ensure that the player achieves meaningful results from the coaching	Following interest Using the GROW model and the Model T Setting goals
Building relationship	To create an environment in which the player feels safe and unjudged	Generating understanding (as above) Creating a contract
Understanding organisational context	To ensure that the coaching engagement meets the client's needs	Generating understanding (as above) Hypothesising/testing hypotheses

Diagram 5. Coaching skills and intents.

other sets fall most easily into other chapters. Let me tell you where you can find them in this book. Chapters 6 and 7 are devoted to generating understanding/raising awareness and proposing respectively. Managing self is included in Chapter 12, 'The art of coaching.' Structuring is divided between a number of chapters: following interest is in Chapter 4, the GROW model and The Model T are described in Chapter 3, and setting goals is in Chapter 9. The building relationship skill set contains the skills of generating understanding/raising awareness on the basis that little builds a relationship more quickly than the experience of being understood. Creating a contract with the player helps ensure a good working relationship and is covered in Chapter 9. Lastly, understanding organisational context has a chapter all to itself, Chapter 11.

THE NOTION OF INTENT

Let me explain what I mean by intent in relation to the skills of coaching and how by understanding this you can learn to be more effective. Skills are the stuff of the 'outer game' as are behaviours and competencies. They can be described and measured and you get a sense of what is to be done. But the notion of 'competencies', so beloved by those who would re-engineer our organisations, is insufficient to our task. This is because it gives you no idea of when or why to deploy the skill or behaviour or, critically, to what effect. I may know quite well that a particular style of question, say an open question, is a useful tool, but if I deploy it indiscriminately I will not help the player. If the skills are of the outer game then there is a corresponding inner game. Real effectiveness lies in understanding both the inner and outer components. In training coaches and linemanagers, I frequently observe them at work. When I notice that they have asked a question or made an intervention that does not seem to help the player I invariably ask 'What was your intent?'.

'Intent' is the inner game of the right question, skill or competency. By intent I mean the purpose or aim of the coach when deploying one or more of the skills. In coaching (and not just in coaching) understanding one's own intent at any moment is a key component in becoming more effective. When I ask novice coaches the intent question I get many kinds of answers. Mostly they point to the coach's need to solve, to fix, to heal, to be right or to be in control; the intentions seldom help the player become more aware or retain responsibility. The following snippet is not untypical:

PLAYER (IN A WORKSHOP)   As I see it there are two things I can do. I can ask my manager to review the decision or I can do what I think is best and hope he doesn't find out.

COACH IN TRAINING   Have you thought of involving the rest of the team?

PROGRAMME LEADER TO COACH   What is your intent with this question?

COACH   Well, the two options are a bit risky and I think he needs to find another approach.

PROGRAMME LEADER   So there are two parts to this; that you think it's risky and that you think he needs another approach. So what specifically is your intent?

COACH   I guess I was trying to steer him towards what I think he should do.

PROGRAMME LEADER   What might be a more appropriate intent?

COACH   First to help him assess the possible risks in the approaches he's identified and then, if the risks are great, to think through other options.

PROGRAMME LEADER   So what's the question for the player?

COACH   I could ask him what might happen if he pursued either of the approaches he identified.

In being clear about the intent, the coach tends to ask more effective questions. But understanding one's intent gives you more than that: it also speaks directly to Self Two and thus enables questions to flow with little or no effort and with great accuracy. And it's so much more fun.

Chapter 6

Generating understanding/raising awareness

This chapter concerns one of the skill sets shown in the chart in the previous chapter. These skills are at the core of effective coaching. Not being proficient in these skills is not an option for a coach.

In this skill set the intent is to help the player understand themself and their situation more fully so that they can make better decisions than they would have done anyway. Notice that I have not said the right decision. When I first came upon *The Inner Game of Tennis* I was very excited and gave it to my mother to read. She had been a successful tennis player and I wanted her to understand my excitement. She took the book away and read it. On returning it to me her comment was, 'I did not understand a word of it, but if it makes a difference to you that is all that matters.' I will not accuse her of being disingenuous but she clearly had understood something; it may not be the 'right' thing or decision from a given perspective, but if it enables the player to move forward and learn and does not damage them or the interests of the organisation then far better to let the player pursue it. The primary function of the coach is to understand. Not to solve, fix, heal, make better or be wise. To understand. The magic is that it is in that moment of understanding that the player understands for himself, becomes more aware and is then in a position to make better decisions and choices than he would have done anyway. This is how coaching is profoundly simple and simply profound. But most of us struggle to get above our own agenda and want to be seen to be making a difference.

The following are the specific skills of generating understanding/raising awareness:

- Listening to understand
- Repetition, paraphrasing, summarising
- Grouping
- Silence
- Asking questions that follow interest
- Asking questions to clarify.

In the following sections I describe each of the specific skills in some depth.

LISTENING TO UNDERSTAND

In this relationship between you and me the closest we can get to the experience of listening is your attending to the words on the page. A blank page would be the closest that I could get to silence within the confines of a book. As you looked at this blank page it is my guess that your experience is not of blankness but rather of all the ideas that you could read into the page. 'Is this a mistake?' 'What a waste of paper!' 'Have I missed something?' In effect you fill the page for me with your own thoughts. As another example, next time you are in a position where someone else is speaking, take the opportunity to notice your own listening. If you are like the rest of us, the quality will be inconsistent and probably dependent on your level of interest in what is being said. In some moments your attention will be completely with the speaker, in others it will drift. Your attention may be held by some particular point that you relate to some other matter … and all of a sudden you are away with the fairies. Perhaps the speaker is a little boring. Or maybe they don't express themselves well. Your judgements creep in. Followed, in short order, by your expectations, opinions and assumptions. Even as you read this page your thoughts might spin off in some flight of fantasy, or something in the environment will distract you. Listening is a fundamental skill, paying attention should be easy. Sometimes in a workshop I will give the participants a simple listening exercise to do. When the exercise is over I will ask them what got in the way of their listening – what were the interferences – and will note down their responses. This is a typical list:

- Other people talking
- What I thought they were going to say
- What I thought they should say
- They were boring
- I had already worked out what they should do
- I had thought of what they were saying already
- What I was thinking was more interesting
- Thinking of the next question
- Thinking of my response
- What's for dinner?
- Why is he wearing that tie?

That little voice in the head works overtime, and it is difficult to stop. Mostly this noise comes directly from Self One and has no earthly use. There is so much going on in our own minds that to make sufficient space for another is difficult. At this point in the workshop some participants get upset. You see, they value their own thoughts and ideas, are entertained by their assumptions and revel in their judgements. Which is fine, of course, as long as they do not try to coach someone or pretend that they are listening.

Forgive me for repeating myself. In coaching the purpose of listening is to understand, because that in turn generates understanding and awareness in the player. Many of us listen not with the intention to understand but with the intention to respond; we are just waiting for the speaker to take a breath so that we can get to speak or, almost as bad, using the time when the other is speaking to think up the next question or a suitable response. In doing some work with an international consultancy some years ago, where the consultants were renowned for their intelligence, a senior partner informed me that 'people around here don't listen, they re-load!'. There is another way; imagine a spring-loaded stack of plates as you might find in a canteen. As you take the top plate the next one is pushed up. Each plate represents an idea or notion that rises into the consciousness of the player. As a thought enters the consciousness and is passed on to a listener the space for the next thought is created. And that one is passed on, and then the next one. Somewhere down in the player's stack of plates, in their mind, is their solution, their creative idea, their insight. If someone is willing to listen then the player may get to that plate, that thought. And because the thought is uniquely theirs they will nurture it, develop it and put it to some creative use.

On the other hand, if the coach takes the first few plates, assumes that he now understands and then gives the player back the plates and then a few more of his own, his own good ideas, his way forward, no real learning has occurred and the player does not own the outcome. And if the coach is also the line-manager, not only is the solution, idea or insight further down the stack, but also in order to get to it the player has to challenge the line-manager's authority. Another good idea lost, another breakthrough unheard – and a demotivated employee.

There are a number of things you can do to improve your listening. The first is simple but not necessarily easy. Start noticing when you are not listening and gently bring your attention back to the speaker. This has one major flaw as a tactic in that the only time you become aware that you have 'gone away with your thoughts' is

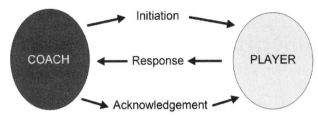

Diagram 6. The coaching communication cycle.

when you return or when the speaker gives you some feedback – which may be too late. If this does happen the only thing to do that has any integrity is to own up. It is unlikely that they will be surprised; they will have noticed, probably before you did.

The second is a discipline called 'managing your communication cycles'. I find this particularly useful when demonstrating coaching in public. The potential for distraction is so great and nerves so a-jangle that I need something quite overt to keep me focused.

The Communication Cycle shown in Diagram 6 is used to help you manage conversations in which there is a need for a high order of understanding. You do not need to do this for every conversation; indeed if you did you would exhaust yourself and those around you.

A prerequisite for communication is a minimum of two people, in this case a coach and a player. The first part of the cycle is called *initiation*: the coach asks a question or issues an instruction to the player. The second part is called the *response*, the player having understood the initiation answers. The answer must be congruent with the initiation.

COACH   Tell me how you got on with your action plan from our last session. [initiation]

PLAYER   I had a truly miserable week. One of my clients pulled out of a deal at the last minute and … [incongruent response]

COACH   I'm sorry, we can return to that if you want, but tell me how
did the action plan go?

PLAYER   Oh, the action plan, I got most of it done, I'd say ninety
percent. I couldn't complete writing up my career vision because I
ran out of time. Not bad, considering the difficulties. [congruent
response]

However, the cycle is not complete here. The cycle is only complete
when the player knows that he has been understood. So the final part
is called *acknowledgement*. At the start of a session, particularly with a
new client, the acknowledgement will take the form of a full summary or paraphrasing of what has been said. This is because the
coach needs to be absolutely certain that he has understood. It is also
because the player needs reassuring that he has been understood.

COACH   Let me check that I've understood. Despite some difficulties, you got ninety percent of the action plan done. The bit you did
not quite finish was your career vision because you ran out of time.
Is that right? [acknowledgement]

As the session progresses and trust develops in the relationship the
need to summarise or paraphrase diminishes. You will still need to
manage your communication cycles but now 'I understand', a grunt
or a nod of the head signals the acknowledgement. Another way to
signal that you have understood is to ask a further question congruent with the response.

COACH   Tell me about the difficulties. [Congruent question/initiation]

The cycle completes and a new one starts. This may seem like a
tedious process to engage in and I would not recommend you use
it while discussing the weather with your neighbour as it will drive
both of you mad and rapidly diminish the number of your friends

and acquaintances. Only use it when there is a need for high quality communication, such as in coaching. As with the GROW model, I would like you to know that for the most part it happens quite naturally and is typically unnoticed by the player. Their experience is of being completely understood, probably for the first time. This builds trust in the relationship and raises awareness but it also does one other thing. It is also a bit like using the 'save' key on your computer; all the important information is now safely stored (understood) so the player can feel free to move on to the next point. It can thus create a flow in the conversation not unlike the earlier image of the stack of plates.

From my own experience I know that when engaging with a new client, with a difficult issue, it is the discipline of managing the communication cycles that has generated real understanding and been the foundation of a successful conversation.

REPEATING, SUMMARISING AND PARAPHRASING

Powerful aspects of generating understanding/raising awareness are repetition, summarising and paraphrasing. And let me remind you again of the intent: to help the player understand themselves and their situation more fully so that they can make better decisions than they would have done anyway. In using these skills something special can happen. As the coach repeats what has been said, summarises, or paraphrases, the player often has a new insight or idea. I can only guess as to why that might happen. I think it is that, as the player hears the issue played back, it is possible to get a little distance (I refer to distance later in this chapter) from the issue, to be not so attached, and in seeing it differently to have some new thoughts. You might have noticed that it is always easier to solve someone else's problem, when there really is distance.

Repetition or repeating verbatim gives a clear signal to the player that you have at least heard the words. But a tape-recorder can do that. What it does not do is signal that you have fully understood. However, it has its place in coaching when a particular set of words, or a word, has significance for the player. This is even more important when there is an emotional undertone. That you have picked up on that significance is a demonstration that you have understood.

COACH   If I remember correctly, earlier in the conversation you said that the team's decision 'didn't just upset me but destroyed my self-confidence'.

PLAYER   Exactly, and it is both of those things, they are both important to sort out.

Summarising is to present in shortened form or to extract the essence and is another demonstration that you have understood.

Paraphrasing differs in that you knowingly choose to substitute your own words or word for the player's. You might do this to check your own understanding or because you believe that the new word or words are in fact a better expression of what the player means. In the coach's role it is a great way of checking that you have actually understood.

In coaching these tools are best used to check understanding, for example after the player has made a number of points or at the end of a stage of the GROW model. Another effective way to use them is to turn them around and have the player summarise or paraphrase. It can generate great clarity of what is truly important for the player. It is also a good trick if you have lost the thread and either have not the courage to own up or deem it inappropriate: 'There was a lot there. Could you summarise it for me?'.

GROUPING

Grouping or chunking is the ability to identify the principal themes or elements or chunks of a conversation and to play these back to the player. Doing this typically has the effect of increasing understanding, and that is indeed the intent. Sometimes in coaching the player is confronted with a problem of magnitude and complexity. It occurs to them as an undifferentiated mess; pea soup. If the coach can identify the various elements, it makes understanding easier: 'So far you've mentioned stock, cream, herbs – but you did not say which herbs – and, of course, peas.

In the coaching conversation in Chapter One, Henry had been speaking for quite some time before Melanie summarises:

'Then, if I have understood, there are three parts to this: the ability of the project team, a shift in the financial parameters, and the differing needs of our two friends, Steve and Jeremy.'

'That's right. Although, on the third point, it's as much about the pressure they put on me as it is about their "needs", as you put it?'

'OK. So four things then, including the pressure they are putting on you. Which would be most interesting to talk about first?'

At its most complex, grouping involves the ability to differentiate and to see that things belong to the same set. To continue the culinary metaphor: 'You have mentioned the vegetables and the fruit. In the vegetable category you have cabbages and carrots and in the fruit category you have oranges, apples and pears.'

SILENCE

Novice coaches are often afraid of silences in their coaching conversations and will jump in with another question. A lot of valuable reflection can be lost when this happens. Silence is truly golden in coaching. Typically it means that the player is busy thinking or processing something for himself. When he is ready he will tell you. There is of course another kind of silence that occurs when the player does not know what he is supposed to be doing, in which case move the session on. It is usually pretty easy to tell when someone is thinking something through (lots of eye movement, concentration) and when they're not (vacant look, distraction), so look for the physical signals.

ASKING QUESTIONS THAT FOLLOW INTEREST

Another way of deepening understanding, and thereby raising awareness, is to ask questions.

We looked at 'asking questions that follow interest' in Chapter Four where I also linked it with the Model T and so there is no need to repeat the information here. But to reinforce the notion of intent I will suggest that this skill is a way of enabling the player to move forward as a function of his or her own thinking and choices. It is non-directive coaching at its best. In following interest the player becomes very focused thus removing interference and in turn allowing full access to their intelligence, imagination and intuition.

Questions that clarify

The W questions – what, who, where and when – are all useful in raising awareness. And then an H question: **How** or **How much**. Notice that I have not included **why**. I'll come back to that shortly.

What, or better still '*what specifically is that*', is useful when someone uses a word that you have not come across before.

PLAYER   And so, without telling anyone, they removed all the codals.

COACH   What specifically is a codal?

(I cannot take this example any further because in order to make the point I had to find a noun that no one would know. So I had to make one up: codal – it's a made-up word.)

In most meetings it would not be the end of the world if you did not understand a particular word. You would merely wait for the break and ask a trusted colleague. In a coaching session, where what drives the session is understanding, you simply cannot afford to miss the meaning. 'What' is also useful when a player uses a word that you do recognise:

PLAYER   In this company I get absolutely no acknowledgement.

COACH   What do you mean by acknowledgement?

PLAYER   A little bit of praise now and again.

You see, everyone else thought that the salary was acknowledgement enough.

Who is useful in two ways. The first way to use it is when someone uses a pronoun (he, she, they, it) and you are not sure who is being referred to.

PLAYER   He said to her that they should all do it together.

COACH   Let me just check that. Who specifically said it? To whom? Who specifically are they? And what is it that they should do?

Just don't ask all the questions at once.

The second way is to get a complete list of all the characters that might have impact on the topic of the coaching conversation: 'Who else is involved?' 'Who are the other members of the team?'.

Where and **when** give specific location in time and place:

PLAYER   I am completely stuck with this report.

COACH   Where exactly in the report are you stuck?

PLAYER   Well, the main part of it is fine, I'm just having difficulty in drawing out the conclusions for the summary.

In this example a worry gets identified as something very specific and the coaching can proceed.

PLAYER   I'll talk to Paul soon.

COACH   When exactly?

PLAYER   Tomorrow, before twelve.

And in this example a loose commitment that could easily be misunderstood (soon could be a few minutes or a few weeks) becomes a firm agreement.

How is a useful question. It is always used in connection with verbs – 'doing' words. It gets to high quality information very quickly. I learned this in a somewhat painful manner as the following anecdote shows.

Charles was my early mentor. We travelled around the UK together for a couple of years, running coaching workshops. This was my apprenticeship. There was, however, a problem associated with all this travel. When I left home to go to a workshop I would upset the balance and dynamics and so was not entirely popular – I would also like to think that I was missed. When I was away another routine was established so my return also upset this. Doubly unpopular. And on my return I was typically exhausted and incapable of normal human interaction. So I asked Charles, he being older and wiser than I, if there was anything I could do to overcome this problem. Charles looked at me and said

'Sinead and I, we rebop.' 'What specifically is that?', I asked. Charles was just getting on a train and responded through the open window in the door, 'It's a semi-erotic, semi-therapeutic activity for two consenting adults.'

By the time I realised that I was really none the wiser it was too late; the train had pulled out of the station. I had made a fundamental mistake; I had asked the **what** question (for nouns) when I should have asked a **how** question. By the time I next met up with Charles I had worked it out: 'Charles, how do you do that, rebop?'. However, Charles was in a taciturn mood and asked me if I was a catholic. I was not but had been brought up as one. Given that and the fact that I was not then married to my now wife, Jo, Charles said he could not, in all conscience, tell me!

As I have said, the 'What' question refers to nouns, the 'How' to verbs. Ask the right question and you get high quality information, thus contributing to understanding. For example:

PLAYER   I need to learn how to manage my team better.

COACH   How do you learn?

PLAYER   I'm not sure. I like to watch others and read a bit. And then I like to give it a go.

The player has pretty much defined an action plan in response to one simple question.

How much adds clarity and raises awareness when matters of quantity, size or scale are under discussion.

PLAYER   We are almost certainly going to fall short of the budgeted target for sales.

COACH   By how much?

A response such as

PLAYER   Only by 3 percent.

is very different from

PLAYER   I guess it could be as much as $200,000.

Depending on the scale of the issue the coaching will follow very different paths.

There is another version of the 'how much' question that has a very similar intent: to raise awareness.

PLAYER   I am really concerned about the new strategy Bob presented yesterday.

COACH   How concerned, on a scale of one to ten?

PLAYER   That's a good question. Actually only about three or four.

COACH   So do we need to discuss it now?

PLAYER   No, it's more important that we talk through the conference.

If the response to the 'how much' question had been eight, then no doubt the coach and player would have talked about Bob's new strategy.

I excluded 'Why' from my list of questions that clarify. The **why** question more often than not elicits reasons, justifications and excuses, not one of which is useful in raising awareness. 'Why' does not create distance. Also, 'why' is a pretty sloppy question. It can mean so many things, from what is your purpose, to what is your reason, to blame as in 'But why?'. So ask a more specific question:

'What is your purpose in that?'
'What were the reasons behind that decision?'
'What is it that makes that important for you?'

Some other questions

I want to include some further types of question for which I could find no obvious category but which can be very effective. One of the mistaken impressions that people get in being introduced to the notion of non-directive coaching is that the coach has to be gentle with the player, that the coach cannot get tough. Tying players down to specifics and getting them to commit are parts of the toolkit. These are aspects of the skill of challenging which I address in Chapter 7.

(1) Get specific.

PLAYER   Well, that has been a useful conversation. I'll try a couple of the things we discussed over the next few weeks.

COACH   Great. Tell me, what specifically you are going to do? And by when?

(2) Commit.

PLAYER   I think I might have a go at giving Paul some feedback.

COACH   You sound a little unsure. What are you actually going to do?

Lastly, before we move on I would like to remind you of the description of the ball-catching demonstration in Chapter 2. Peter's natural ability to catch manifested when he was focused, when there was no interference. It's the same for you as a coach. If you are completely focused and interested in your player's learning, your natural instinct to coach – Self Two – will manifest, and you will ask an appropriate question. In any case it does not particularly matter if you make a mistake. Coaching is not an exam where you get only one chance. If a question does not work, ask another. When you are in a good relationship it does not matter. There is only one mistake that you can make in coaching and that is to irreparably damage the relationship.

Finally in this section on questions, please do not worry about the 'right' question to ask; do not get stuck in your doubts or the models, simply get interested; if you're stuck your attention is with you and not with the player. One of the best questions I was ever asked when I was being coached went like this:

BEN   I don't know what the next question is. Do you?

And of course I did.

POSTSCRIPT

The issue of distance, which is referred to a little earlier in this chapter, is important in coaching. If a player is caught up in a difficult or emotional topic there is no distance. He really is the problem. I remember sitting on the top deck of a London bus travelling into the West End in heavy traffic. As the bus approached a junction I could see, before it actually happened, that we were heading for a complete logjam. Four cars at the junction had managed to get into positions from which none could easily move. From the top of the bus it was easy to see the solution. If the blue car just pulled back a few feet that would allow the red car … . However, for the driver of the blue car it is a different matter. He gets angry and frustrated: 'Just what I need when I'm late. Where did that @★^! > in the red car come from? Shouldn't be allowed on the road …'. He has become the problem. If he could only see it – the logjam and himself, from the top of the bus – he might also see the solution. It is the job of the effective coach to get the player – the driver in this analogy – out of the jam and up onto the top of the bus and get some distance. I used the jigsaw analogy in the description of the GROW model. This is the same thing – it is what I mean by raising awareness. The process of talking to the coach and then of good reflecting back, through either summarising or the gentle raising of an eyebrow, of simply being understood, can create that distance.

The skills described in this chapter are those of generating understanding/raising awareness and are all situated at the non-directive end of the range of coaching approaches. The intent that I ascribed to this skill set is 'to help the player understand themself and their situation more fully so that they can make better decisions.' In the next chapter we slide a little to the left of the range, towards the more directive skills, but with caution.

Chapter 7
Proposing

I approach this chapter with the tiniest degree of trepidation. My concern is that, in devoting a whole chapter to the skills at the directive end of the range of coaching approaches, I might be seen to be giving equal weight to these skills. This is not what I intend to communicate. In any coaching conversation I spend approximately eighty percent of the time at the non-directive end of the range, those of generating understanding/raising awareness, because that is what is most effective. There are occasions in coaching – and always fewer than you think – where the coach has something of value to add. This set of skills, which I call proposing, is perhaps the most difficult skill set to apply *effectively* because of the inherent dangers of removing responsibility and choice from the player. The paradox is that it is the traditional model and where we typically begin. Towards the end of the chapter I have included a short section on 'Transparency' to help overcome this difficulty and also put forward four tests for the coach to apply when about to propose.

Proposing is a different skill set from generating understanding/raising awareness as it covers the skills involved when the coach chooses to make an input, rather than drawing information from the player. In Chambers Dictionary the definition of the word 'propose' is given as 'to put forward or exhibit, to bring to one's own or another person's attention'. The latter part of the definition is particularly appropriate as it acknowledges that while the coach may, for example, make a suggestion, the player does not have to include it in his thinking or act on it. To propose is not to impose. Let me remind you of the intent in proposing. It is *to make available to the player the coach's observations, knowledge, experience, intelligence, insight, intuition and wisdom*. However, the result is ultimately the same as for generating understanding/raising awareness: to help the player understand themself and their situation more fully so that they can make better decisions than they would have done otherwise.

The following are the specific skills of proposing and I describe them in detail in this chapter:

- Giving feedback
- Making suggestions
- Giving advice
- Instructing
- Challenging
- Evoking creativity
- Transparency.

GIVING FEEDBACK

Unfortunately giving and receiving feedback is optional. I know it could not be any other way, but you have only to ask two questions of people in most organisations to be very clear that there is not a whole lot of giving and receiving feedback happening.

The first question is 'Have you given any feedback recently?', to which the answer is almost always 'yes'. Then you ask 'Have you received any feedback recently?', to which the answer is invariably 'no'. If you ask these questions across an organisation you can form a number of hypotheses, one of which is that there is an incredibly sorted person – who you have missed because they are locked up in the basement - who is getting all the feedback. Another is that not much feedback is happening. A third, and more generous one, is that people think they are giving feedback when in fact they are alluding to something or dropping hints. Whichever is the case the vast majority of us do not receive sufficient feedback.

This is an important issue. The body–mind is a cybernetic system. That is to say, it requires feedback from its environment in order to function properly. Another example of a cybernetic system is a guided missile – a bit out of place in this book, perhaps (resorting to violence does rather fall off the directive end of the range of coaching approaches), but it makes the point. A guided missile requires feedback to know whether it is on target or not.

A sensory deprivation chamber, or float tank, is a place where the body–mind gets virtually no feedback and it is useful to look at what happens if someone is left in such a place for too long. A float tank is a bit like a bath, only bigger, usually about seven or eight feet square. It is filled to a depth of about eighteen inches with a high-density saline solution that is exactly at body temperature. It is totally enclosed. No light gets in and no sound. You cannot feel anything much because you are floating and you do not notice the water because it is at exactly the same temperature as your skin. In short your senses are deprived of all or almost all stimulation. It is a sensory deprivation chamber. An hour spent in a float tank gives you the equivalent rest to seven hours' sleep and is a powerful rejuvenating process. It can also put the mind in an extremely receptive state. Many people have solved nagging or serious problems, or had a creative idea in a float tank. Some sports people use them in conjunction with video. In this receptive state they see images of themselves performing perfectly and thus train the muscle memory to repeat perfect performances. All very good, as long as you do not mind smelling faintly of epsom salts for a week. However if you stay in the float tank for too long you begin to hallucinate – you make it up. After a while you go mad. There are lots of people walking around organisations who are hallucinating; many of them are senior executives to whom nobody feels able to tell the truth. The consequence of not receiving feedback is that we make it up. You know that report that someone left on your desk last week, the one that you have not had time to read. Let me tell you that they have already made up what happened: it was not good enough. And what can follow from 'it was not good enough' is often 'I am not good enough'. Let me say it again: when people do not know what the reality is, they make it up.

At workshops it is a useful thing to do to ask people what stops them from giving feedback. A typical list includes some of these ideas:

- It's not part of my job.
- If they can't do the job they should not be here.
- It's not in the culture.
- I don't have time.
- I don't have enough information.
- Who am I to judge another.
- I don't want to discourage them.
- I don't want to hurt them.

When pushed, most will acknowledge that not giving feedback comes down to 'I don't want to hurt them'. Underneath 'I don't want to hurt them' is another issue that I think it's worth being really clear about. And it is this: if I hurt you, you will not like me any more. An understandable, but hardly noble, reason for withholding feedback.

Imagine this scenario. A chair and, behind it about fifteen feet away, a waste-paper basket. In the chair sits an unsuspecting volunteer. His task, the coach informs him, is to throw a ball over his head so that it lands in the basket. It must go straight in and not bounce in. And no looking. The coach's job is to give the volunteer feedback. The player throws a ball.

COACH   You missed.

PLAYER   Really.

COACH   Have another go.

Another attempt.

COACH   You missed again.

PLAYER   By how much?

COACH   Listen, sunshine, I'm in a hurry. Get on with it.

Another attempt.

COACH   That was even worse.

PLAYER   What do you want me to do?

COACH   Just get the ball in the basket. I suppose it's worth another
try.

Eventually in exasperation the player throws the ball at the coach.
   This conversation is noticeable for

- The judgemental attitude of the coach
- The coach's lack of belief in the player's ability
- The coach making no attempt to create a relationship
- No usable data from the coach.

What is most worrying is that I occasionally demonstrate the con-
versation above in workshops and some participants start laughing.
They can identify with the style only too well.
   So the coach has learned his lesson and tries again.

COACH   Thanks for volunteering. It's David, isn't it?

DAVID   Yes.

COACH   The exercise remains the same and I'm wondering what you would like me to do to help.

DAVID   I'd like some real feedback.

COACH   And what exactly would you like from me?

DAVID   I'd like to know how far the ball was from the basket.

COACH   OK. And anything else?

DAVID   I guess you could tell me if it landed in front or behind the basket. And on which side.

COACH   OK. In front or behind and the side. How should I tell you how far away?

DAVID   What do you mean?

COACH   Feet, feet and inches, metres, that sort of thing.

David   Oh no, I'm no good with distances. Just show me with your hands.

COACH   Ready to try?

DAVID   Yes.

David throws.

COACH   The ball landed in front of the bucket, about this much [shows with hands] and about the same distance to the left.?

Within minutes David will throw a ball in the basket. This conversation is noticeable for

- A non-judgemental approach – just the data
- High quality data
- Feedback in the form the player wanted it
- A stronger relationship
- The coach's belief in the player's potential (you'll have to take my word for it).

Before we go any further I want to put something to bed. There is no such thing as negative feedback and there is no such thing as positive feedback. There is just feedback – data. What happens is that people attach a judgement to the data to suit their purpose in that moment. That purpose is usually 'to be right'. And then the receiver responds to the judgement and not to the data. 'The boss is angry so I won't do that again' is not a great way of getting to a good decision. The role of the coach is to give the data as cleanly as possible, so that the player can receive it, assess it and make their own decision as to how to proceed.

That said, in giving feedback it is nigh impossible to communicate only the data. The receiver will also get some sense of your intent and the emotional charge that you carry. We must distinguish carefully between these three aspects of feedback:

- **Data** needs to be of the highest quality you can identify, the more specific the better. It also needs to be something that you have observed – second-hand information frustrates people because they cannot effectively challenge it. Examples help. Keep it free from judgement and interpretation.
- **Intent.** You must be really clear about your intent in giving the feedback. If it is to prove yourself right or to get one up on the receiver it will not work. The only intent that has integrity is to raise awareness.
- **Emotional charge.** Are you angry, disappointed, elated? Whatever your emotions are, they will communicate to some degree. You simply cannot help it. It is often useful to acknowledge this explicitly so that you can manage yourself better.

Giving feedback in everyday work life

There is a useful three-step process to remember for giving feedback in the course of everyday work life:

- Contract
- Data
- Action.

Contract refers to the agreement you make with the person to whom you wish to give feedback. Ideally the contract includes an **offer** and **clarity of intent**.

COACH   I have some feedback for you. Do you want it?

Usually the answer is 'yes'. If it is 'no', it might be appropriate to check the reason behind the rejection of the offer.

COACH   I appreciate that you don't want my feedback. May I ask why?

PLAYER   I'm really busy right now; could we speak later?

Or

PLAYER   This is not a good place; it's too public. Can we use your office?

If, however, the coach is also the line-manager and the offer of feedback has been turned down and it is a critical, management issue, the line-manager might have to insist on giving the feedback: 'I appreciate that you are not interested in my feedback, but it is my view that your approach to these meetings is jeopardising the whole project. So I have a responsibility to give you the feedback. Do you want to have it now or later?'.

The second element, clarity of intent, has already been demonstrated in the previous example. Another example is 'I want to make sure you are successful in running these meetings'.

As mentioned above, **data** should be of the highest quality possible, observed and owned by you, without judgement or interpretation. If it is a weighty matter then at this point you might ask the player to self-assess 'How do you see it?'.

Subsets of the data step are situation, behaviour and impact: 'In this afternoon's meeting about the Odyssey Project, when you questioned Jack [situation] I thought you were a little abrupt with him [behaviour]. He seemed to me to be upset and demotivated as a result [impact].'

The feedback will almost certainly be ineffectual if there is neither clarity nor agreement about the **action** the player will do next. If it is a complex issue, the player may require further coaching, though you should not assume that you will be the coach. However, a simple question will typically be sufficient: 'How might you help Jack get motivated again?'. More generic examples include: 'How could you approach this kind of situation in the future?' and 'How, specifically, will you take this forward from here?'.

Giving feedback in a coaching session

Many of the guidelines suggested above hold true for giving feedback in a coaching session. It is still important that the coach does not make an assumption that the player will welcome the feedback. If the session has been run in a non-directive fashion and, suddenly and uninvited, the coach comes out with some feedback, it can be very disruptive to the session and can damage the relationship. And without relationship, coaching cannot happen. The key is to offer the feedback, signalling clearly that this is a change of style, and once the feedback has been delivered, to move back into the non-directive mode: 'I've got some feedback for you. Do you want it?', and then

'What I have noticed is …'
'How does that fit in with what you've been saying?'
'Is that worth considering?'.

I have occasionally had a player say 'no' when I have offered feedback. When it does happen it is almost always because they are busy thinking through another part of the issue and do not want that process interrupted. When they are ready, then I give the feedback. If they do not want it – which would be quite strange – do not give it. If a pattern emerges in continually refusing feedback, then the coach might give feedback on the continual refusal.

MAKING SUGGESTIONS

In the context of coaching, suggestions are ideas that I have that I believe to be appropriate to your situation. They arise in my mind as a function of my experience, my intelligence, my intuition or my imagination. They are occasionally valid and occasionally acceptable to the player. As with feedback the only issue is whether I can present them to the player in such a way as to give the player a genuine choice as to whether to accept them or not. The issue of choice can be influenced by a number of factors; my power in the relationship, my ability to influence, the player's desire to be influenced or to not have to take responsibility. There is a complexity here that no amount of words written can completely resolve, so let us return to what you can do. The guidelines are not dissimilar to those for offering feedback:

- Always present your suggestions as an offer: 'I've got a suggestion would you like to hear it?'
- When the suggestion has been heard, return to the non-directive approach: 'Does that work for you?' or 'We've identified a number of suggestions – w, x, y and the one I threw in, z. Which of those is the most interesting?'.

GIVING ADVICE

I have some problems with offering advice in a coaching session. It seems to me that offering advice suggests that the player and the coach do not see the situation from the same place. Advice suggests that the coach has not really been helpful in taking the player through the reality stage of the GROW model. When I give advice I am making a stand for what I believe in and have probably stopped attending to the player's learning. So I tend not to give it. I am, of course, presenting a rather narrow interpretation of advice. If you find yourself in the position of giving advice, the guidelines are the same as for any time you move from a non-directive mode. Make an offer and, if the advice is wanted, give it. Once it has been heard return to the non-directive mode so the player is left with choice.

INSTRUCTING

Giving instructions is sometimes appropriate in coaching sessions. What it implies is that there is a technique or approach that the coach knows and that the player could not work out for himself, or that it would take more time for the player to work it out than is available. As a tennis coach I knew quite a bit about how to play tennis, the proper technique and way of doing it. Mostly it just got in the way of the player's learning. These are some of the times when instructions might be appropriate:

- When the player is tired
- When there is significant time pressure
- When the player is upset or panicking
- When the technique is complex (and known to the coach).

If you must give instructions, get permission to do so first and then return to the non-directive mode. In my experience 99 percent of the times when I have resorted to giving instructions it is because I, as the coach, have lost my way in the session, or lost interest or was just too tired.

The reality of course is that you can tell anyone to do anything. They just may not do it. Some people may sometimes do what you say, but that is because either they have surrendered their authority to you or they are unwilling to challenge your right to instruct, in which case we could not call it a coaching session. Very occasionally, I have told people what to do in a coaching session, but always with explicit permission. And, as far as I can remember, it is always when the player is so overwhelmed that he needs another to take control for a short while. That is OK as long as it does not then result in the player becoming dependent on the coach.

CHALLENGING

I have put this specific skill in the proposing section although it could just as well sit in the generating understanding/raising awareness section. For although challenging arises from the coach's understanding, its function is to raise awareness. True challenge comes from a belief in potential. I remember coaching a senior manager in a large, UK retail organisation. Mike was given a project to restructure a major division of the organisation, which would lead to some redundancies, but there were no clear objectives behind the project. When I asked how he could identify some, Mike said he could talk with his manager, who had given him the task. I asked him when he might do this. We were sitting across a table in a small meeting room. Mike had virtually collapsed in his chair and looked as if the air had been sucked out of him.

> 'I don't know that I want to go through all the trouble.'
> 'Why not?'

'I am thinking of leaving the business.'

'You're thinking of this – or you've decided?'

'I am not sure.'

At this point I became really clear. Here was a highly intelligent and caring man who had given up. This was not a person acting to his potential. So I challenged:

'Listen, if you don't get clear objectives from your boss you immediately eliminate one option from your choices – because if you're not successful in this project you could lose your job. Tell me, how are you going to get clear objectives for the restructuring?'

He sat up and we talked through his options. When that part of the conversation was complete I then asked him how he would go about deciding whether to stay in the organisation or not. Further action steps emerged. Mike left the meeting walking on air. Sure, nothing had been resolved but he was now, to some degree, in control. I was unwilling to see him renounce his authority.

In challenging it is particularly important to check your intent. 'Being right' at this moment helps no one. As I said, true challenge comes from a belief in the other's potential.

EVOKING CREATIVITY

Creativity is a vital part of coaching. It is what allows the player to break out of a difficult situation, invent a new future or possibility, and make a step-change in their productivity or quality of life. It shows up in many ways, but the two that we will focus on here are concerned with creating the future (visioning and goal setting) and innovation (new ways of doing things, new options). A third technique, generating success criteria, I describe in Chapter 9 as part of the process of setting goals for a coaching programme.

In many of my coaching sessions I am guilty of accepting what is apparently reasonable, in the sense of what could reasonably be achieved, for instance, when a player is creating a vision for their career. In my mind I very often have an idea of what is possible for that person, what they are capable of achieving. And that set of judgements shows up in the session and has the potential to limit it. What is even more worrying is that my idea of what the player is capable of is often greater than his or her own. The same thing can happen in the options stage of the GROW model. The player comes up with a list of options that is within the confines of what is reasonable and the coach goes along with it. Now, I am not an adherent to that school of thought that says whatever you can dream of you can have. There are some things that limit us – at least in this stage of our evolution. But I am absolutely certain that there is much, much more available to us, if only we dare look.

I use the words 'create the future' with some resistance because I know that there are people out there who think the world is the way it is, that their lot is either predetermined or delivered to them out of chaos. And they have an absolute right to that point of view. As a coach I may of course challenge them on it. For their own sake I would want them to be certain that it was a true belief and not an excuse that allows them to dodge their responsibility for having their life work and to accept the current situation without having to struggle.

This section of the book, then, is about how we can respectfully challenge players, and perhaps ourselves, to look beyond what is merely reasonable and scale the heights of the extraordinary.

Most of us, most of the time, create the future from the past. It is a predictable future. If we are brave we may push the boundaries out a bit and create some 'stretch goals'. But essentially the future we imagine for ourselves is an extrapolation of what went on before. We create the future as a function of our previous experience; what worked and what did not work, our likes and dislikes, our strengths and weaknesses, our successes and failures. Unconscious processes also create needs that demand to be fulfilled. Parents, family and cultural background all play their part. All from the past. And you have to be strong and courageous to do something different – and that is after you have given yourself permission even to imagine something different. The funny thing is that the people who are supposed to have our best interests closest to heart are the people who do the most to ensure that we conform. 'But, dear, we have always thought you would become a doctor, just like your father. Why would you ever want to be a footballer?' (Why indeed?) So is there another way of creating the future? Ultimately, not really, because it is nigh impossible to imagine something that has not had existence. The only question is whether you are willing to be constrained by the past. Can you free yourself sufficiently to create a future that is worth hanging around for, that demands your best efforts? You know what they say. Be careful what you wish for; you may get it.

Coaching techniques for creating the future

The first is the most simple, to create a vision. Agree a time frame that makes sense to the player (the year end, one year, five years, to retirement). Ask the player to think of all the things that might be possible in that time frame. Ask them to suggest as many ideas as they can. That done, ask them to edit the list to what they are willing to commit to.

A second approach is to have the player write a speech that would be given at the completion point of the vision: retirement, the end of a project, New Year's Day. What would be the successes and accomplishments that had occurred?

A third option is to have the player draw a picture of the vision. This can be either abstract, free drawing or a more figurative picture. Obviously some people will find this kind of exercise easier than others. This imagery is then translated by the player into a written or verbal vision or set of goals. However, ensure they hold on to their picture as it will remain a potent symbol.

A final and perhaps least conventional option is to get the player to close their eyes and relax. Ask them to allow an image for the vision to come to them. The first image is usually the most useful. They can then either describe the image to you or draw a picture of it as above.

Coaching techniques for evoking innovation

The following are three simple ways of having a player move beyond what they think is possible and creating some more innovative options.

Brainstorming is the simplest. Get the player to create a list of all the possible options. Somewhat less obvious is to ask: 'If you had a magic wand what would you do?', or 'What is the most outrageous option you can think of?', or perhaps 'Think of something that would be impossible.' Identifying something that is apparently impossible can free up the thinking:

PLAYER   It would be impossible for me to not do the project at all.

COACH   What would be one step less than not doing it at all?

PLAYER   Doing some part of it. Now that I say that, if I just did the initial assessment phase in the next week to ten days my boss would be happy.

TRANSPARENCY AND THE FOUR TESTS

In completing this chapter on the skills of proposing I remind you what the intent behind the skill set is. It is to make available to the player the coach's observations, knowledge, experience, intelligence, insight, intuition and wisdom. I mentioned earlier that these are the most difficult skills to deploy because of the inherent dangers of removing responsibility and choice from the player. There are two techniques that I am aware of that are helpful. One is the idea of transparency, which I also mention in Chapter 9 in the context of building a good working relationship between the coach and the player; the other I call the Four Tests. Transparency in coaching means that one's intentions as the coach are completely clear to the player and, almost certainly, explicitly so. Some examples a coach might use are; 'My intention in giving you this feedback is to help you understand the impact of your behaviour' and 'I really did not understand what you just said. Can you say it again?'.

There is slightly different use of transparency that also helps when proposing. What I suggest is that you signal clearly to the player that you are moving from the non-directive to the directive end of the range. This allows them to know that you are aware that the information is yours and that you do not wish to impose it. For example: 'I have a suggestion for you, another option; do you want it?'. Assuming that he or she does want it then make the suggestion. And having proposed the option, return immediately to the Non-Directive, for example: 'You had two options of your own and then I added one in. Which is most interesting to talk more about?'.

The Four Tests operate in a different way. I will use them in a coaching session when I notice that I have something to propose, such as a suggestion to offer or some feedback. If I am not sure that it is the right thing to do I will ask myself the following questions:

- Will it raise awareness?
- Will it leave responsibility and choice with the player?
- Is the relationship strong enough to withstand the intervention (i.e. is there sufficient trust in my intention)?
- What is my intent?

If the answer to the first three is 'yes' and my intent is congruent with the suggested intent behind this skill set then I will go ahead.

POSTSCRIPT

To finish the chapter I give a cautionary tale. Many years ago I was coaching a senior consultant, we'll call him Mark, in a large management consultancy. After the third meeting I asked for some feedback. In responding he made a request:

MARK   I would like more from you.

MYLES   More what?

MARK   More input, more suggestions and feedback.

In the following session I complied with the request and at the end of the meeting was feeling quite dissatisfied. I could see Mark was too, but on the day I did not have the necessary courage to ask for more feedback. It so happened that on the following day I had to give a demonstration of tennis coaching to a very discerning audience. I knew that if I made the slightest suggestion it would be picked up, so I was determined to be as non-directive as possible. It was a great session and reminded me of what constituted effective coaching. It also caused me to reflect on my coaching of Mark.

Taking a more directive stance had clearly not helped and, as I thought about it, in the earlier meetings I had been too polite with my questioning and had not helped Mark really clarify his thinking. In the next meeting I listened even more intently and made sure that I really understood all he was saying. I applied the GROW model with more precision, making sure to establish a clear outcome from the conversation. We finished our work in less than an hour, about half the normal time. Mark had worked so hard he was almost perspiring. As I left the meeting room, Mark turned and said: 'That was hard work. You really made me think. Thank you.'

Chapter 8
Coaching in the workplace

So far in this book I have covered the underlying principles, key models and many of the skills of effective coaching and I have tried to give a sense of what coaching looks like in practice. In this chapter I intend to show how coaching fits in the organisational context and the line-manager's role. Crucially I want to discuss how to use coaching for the benefit of the organisation and the player. Up till now it has not been necessary to distinguish between the needs of the professional coach and those of the line-manager. As we begin to think about how coaching fits in the workplace it becomes necessary to distinguish between the two roles. So, in this chapter I will present most of the content from the line-manager's perspective. I have chosen to do this not only because it is the primary application of coaching (there are more line-managers than coaches – just about) but also because a professional coach working in organisations needs to have a good understanding of the line-manager's role as most of the people they coach are line-managers. To restore the balance, Chapter 11, 'Coaching in context', is presented from the professional coach's perspective, as the content is a little more pertinent to that audience.

In this chapter I also want to present an argument that concerns the line-manager's role and the place of coaching within it. My desire to do this comes from a recent conversation during a workshop when I asked the participants, all line-managers, what the purpose of line-management was. Specifically, I asked this question:

'When whoever it was invented the notion of line-management, what was the problem they were trying to solve?'. I did not get a very good answer. Indeed, as we discussed it further and notions of coaching emerged, one guy looked up and said 'but this is not how I think of my job.' And there lies the problem. Most managers think of their job in terms of their trade, discipline or profession. The manager title is thought about in terms of status and increased remuneration; it is not really thought about as a new set of responsibilities. My evidence for this assertion is the observation that few managers get out of bed in the morning and think 'what can I do today to help my team be brilliant?'. It's just not their job as they see it. So the argument concerns the nature of line-management and the place of coaching and it starts with some observations about a fundamental dynamic in any work organisation: the relationship between the individual employee and the organisation itself.

THE INDIVIDUAL AND THE ORGANISATION

Individuals join organisations so that they can achieve some of their goals. These goals can be simple: to make enough money to pay the mortgage; or they may be complex: to satisfy their need to make a meaningful contribution. Equally, these goals can be well thought through and clear, or reactive and ambiguous.

Organisations employ individuals so that the organisation can fulfil its mission and achieve its goals. Typically the goals are, if not clear, at least explicit and so those responsible seek people who will fit in, have the right skills and compatible values. Organisations are typically more diligent in identifying the right person then individuals are in identifying the right organisation – or in understanding their own needs and goals.

A successful relationship between an individual and an organisation is achieved when both parties achieve their own goals. This is

Diagram 7. The elements of the line-manager's role.

a fundamental dynamic in any organisation; if it is entirely neglect-
ed people leave and, ultimately, there is no organisation.

The individual has obviously a significant responsibility in
ensuring the success of the relationship, as does the organisation.
The organisation will give authority to a number of people to
ensure that its responsibility is met. Some of this is laid at the door
of the HR professionals. But by far the greatest share of the organisation's responsibility rests with the line-manager. It is their job to
ensure that both parties' needs are satisfied. There are three generic elements to the line-manager's role that enable this to happen:
leadership, management and coaching (Diagram 7).

LEADERSHIP, MANAGEMENT AND COACHING

In the past fifteen years the notion that leadership is part of the line-
manager's role has come to be accepted in most organisations. We
(the world of business and management, that is) have separated out
that part of the role and examined it, defined the component skills,

written them into the job description and the values statements, and created training and development programmes. Now what is emerging is that coaching is another critical element of the line-manager's role. The evidence for this is to be found in the press articles, books and conferences that have proliferated in the last ten years and in the ever-increasing demand for coaching-skills development programmes. And so, in a fashion similar to that in which leadership has been distinguished from management, we need to separate coaching from management and leadership.

Much has been written about leadership and I do not want to get into that discussion here. Suffice it to say that by leadership I mean the element of the role that is concerned with the future. It is concerned with creating a vision, with maintaining that vision and with identifying actions in the present that will deliver the vision. Role modelling fits here too; the living values, and portraying the values of the organisation.

In this model the management element of the role is concerned with ensuring that the subordinate performs their role within certain parameters. These parameters include:

- The type and nature of the organisation's business (an employee of a kitchenware manufacturer cannot, on a whim, start taking orders for a new line of musical instruments)
- The purpose and goals of the organisation
- The requirements of the specific job
- Performance standards; management processes
- The cultural norms and any accepted rules of the company.

As I pointed out in the Introduction, I refer to what we traditionally call 'managers' as 'line-managers'. I do this because 'managing' is a subset of the role; it is not all of it. There is an emerging practice of calling line-managers 'team leaders' or 'coaches'. In many cases, principally where the 'coach' has a management function, this is a mistake as it simply repeats the initial error – defining the role by one of its subsets. In some organisations where there has been an initiative to develop a coaching culture, line-managers have seemingly lost the right to manage; they can only coach, often resulting in a loss of appropriate control and endless conversations on issues that are not negotiable.

Coaching, as I have said before but in other ways, is the series of conversations that help a person perform closer to their potential, understand their role or task, help them learn what they need to learn in order to complete the role or task successfully, develop them for the next role, and on a good day help them achieve fulfilment at work and, maybe, a little joy.

In a workshop I might ask the participants to identify all the activities, interactions and conversations that are the day-to-day content of the three circles of leadership, management and coaching. Here is a typical list:

- Leadership
  - conversations about organisational mission, vision, goals, values
  - role modelling behaviours, values
  - inspiring and motivating.

- Management
  - appraisals
  - setting individual and departmental goals
  - recruitment interviews
  - creating personal development plans
  - agreeing parameters of projects, tasks
  - disciplinary meetings.

- Coaching
  - conversations about how to deliver goals, plans, etc., agreed in a previous management
  - giving feedback, making suggestions, offering advice
  - on-the-job training.

At a recent workshop one of the participants, the Sales Director from a sizeable travel agency chain, literally stood up and declared 'I see, I have one management meeting a year with each member of my team to establish the goals and the rest of the time I coach them to achieve the goals.' He did appreciate that this was something of an over-simplification but he had understood the point and that he needed to invest a greater proportion of his time in coaching. The partner in charge of a major regional head office of one of the Big Four (it may of course be three by the time you read this) accountancies learned something different. He signed out of a workshop with these words: 'You may not have made my life any easier, but you have certainly made it more simple.' He realised that the conversations that he had avoided with his fellow partners concerning the clarification of their business goals and non-performance in relation to them were critical issues to the success of the office. He knew that he had a management task to complete, defining the goals, before coaching became possible. He also did not expect the conversations to be without friction.

There is an interesting paradox here. If people do not have clear goals it is extremely difficult to be successful and even more difficult to discuss performance. Forcing the issue, having the discussion, being really clear about goals and what is acceptable and what is not, removes a mass of interference, removes the ill-feeling that often accompanies under-performance, and enables best performance.

Later in this chapter I will develop this model of leadership, management and coaching, but before I do that I need to introduce the notion of authority as it pertains to organisations.

ORGANISATIONAL AND INDIVIDUAL AUTHORITY

There is an underlying issue here that relates to these three elements. This is the issue of authority. By authority I mean the power to decree something, by right or office, and to get it done by oneself or others. In order to be an effective line-manager it is imperative to understand the nature of authority and where it lies. Misunderstanding these issues will affect performance in a work organisation and is critical to a line-manager's capacity to ensure the satisfaction of both the organisation and the individual employee. Here are some examples.

In the past (I hope), the culture in most organisations was very authoritarian – 'command and control' being the predominant management style. Look at the words we use: 'subordinate' and 'empowerment'. How I hate that latter word. People are by their very nature powerful. That we have to 'empower' them suggests that their power has in some way been diminished or taken away. We have, through our culture, our institutions of state and religion, and particularly our educational systems, trained people to submit to authority. And there are consequences. Under a strongly hierarchical, authoritative 'regime' people do not take responsibility, do not take risks, are not creative, are not proactive. Rather they wait to be told. This is not how to get the best from people – 'our greatest asset'. This is misplaced authority.

On the other hand, many people do not understand that when they join an organisation, they sign up to play in that organisation's 'game' and to play by its rules. I know this because very few people take the time in the recruitment phase to understand the organisation they are joining. The closest most people get to making a real choice is to select a profession or particular industry to work in. Otherwise the agreement around the pay package or salary is about as far as it gets. And, again in most cases, this is perfectly understandable. You've left school, college or university and have debts to pay off. Or there's a family, a mortgage. Pragmatism is the only operable philosophy. It works because the money is sufficient to make it worth staying. So you get on with it, do as you're told and get to pay the bills. Clearly this is not true for everyone. The point

I am trying to make is that most people do not 'stand in their authority', and take responsibility. The consequence of this is people who experience little fulfilment at work, who are thus difficult to motivate and who perform with mediocrity.

I remember giving an address to a conference. The delegates were all senior managers and executives, mostly male and getting towards middle age. These were people who were used to exercising power, many controlling budgets of millions of pounds. So I asked them who made the decision about where they took their holidays in that particular year. There was a short pause and then an embarrassed laugh, no, a giggle, ran around the room. These guys exercised absolutely no authority about how they were going to spend two or three weeks of the year (weeks that they had probably fought hard for in negotiating their salary package). And most of them had gone to places that would not have been their first choice and done things they would not join a queue of two for. And they had not even come to a compromise on the matter – they had simply capitulated. In the name of a quiet life.

Organisations can assume too much authority, individuals too little, although there is a spin on this. I notice that the generation that is currently entering the workforce has a completely different relationship with authority than I, for one, ever did. They are more assertive, assume more 'rights' and are less willing to 'toe the line'. This is in itself a compelling reason to adopt something other than a 'command and control' management style because in a world where attracting the best staff is increasingly an issue, the best will not stay in an unduly authoritarian organisation.

There is an appropriate balance to be struck between individual and organizational authority, and the line-manager, caught in the middle, needs to understand how to strike it. Sometimes individuals get together with other individuals and agree to share authority so that they can achieve something together that they cannot achieve apart. Like a marriage. And in order that it is successful the individual parties have to surrender some of their authority to the whole. Similarly, organisations and individuals can get together. It's a business relationship called employment.

Individuals have authority. By this I mean that there are areas of their lives where they can make decisions and execute them without reference to others. Organisations have authority too. They can declare the business they are in, establish goals and strategies and execute them.

One way to understand how the matter of authority impacts on organisational life is to draw a vertical line through the middle of the three overlapping circles shown in Diagram 7; then you can begin to see where this balance lies. The left-hand side of the line (Diagram 8) represents those things that are the concern of the organisation: it's needs, aims and objectives. On this side of the line the organisation has authority. When you join an organisation you sign up to that authority. The area on the right-hand side of the line

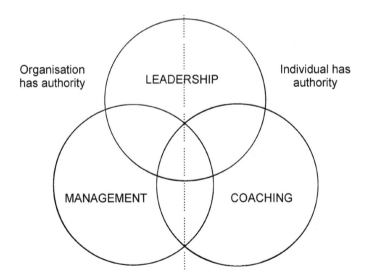

Diagram 8. The elements of the line-manager's role classified according to authority.

represents those things that are the concern of the individual: their needs, aims and objectives. On this side of the line the individual has authority.

It is overly simplistic but nevertheless useful shorthand to suggest that *what* an individual employee does sits on the left-hand side in the authority of the organisation. Clearly this is best agreed (the manager using coaching skills to understand the individual) rather than decreed. *How* the *what* gets executed sits for the most part on the right-hand side of the line, in the authority of the individual employee.

Let me draw a parallel with the game of tennis. When a player stands on a tennis court he implicitly signs up to the rules of the game as laid down by the International Tennis Federation. The player cannot change the size of the court, or the height of the net, or alter the rules. He cannot, for instance, decide to kick the ball. If he does the game ceases to be tennis. In addition to the player there are a number of other people on the tennis court; his opponent, the umpire and the coach. The umpire and the coach are of interest in this analogy, not the opponent. The umpire's role is essentially about compliance. It is his job to ensure that the rules of the game are adhered to. In this sense it is analogous to the management element of the of the line-manager's role. The coach's role is different. His job is to ensure that the player gives his best performance and learns and improves from one match to the next. And it is obviously analogous to the coaching aspect of the line-manager's role.

The very different roles of the umpire and the coach suggest a different kind of relationship with the player, and different corresponding behaviours. The umpire's relationship is invested with authority, given by the governing body. It is a directive, command-and-control interactive style. Appropriately: if the rules were not enforced there would be no game.

The coach's relationship is altogether different. The content of the conversations between the coach and the player concerns matters that are within the authority of the player; whether he hits a backhand with one or two hands on the racket or whether he adopts an aggressive serve-and-volley strategy or a back-court, counter-hitting approach. On the right-hand side of the diagram, where the individual has authority, instructing or telling that individual is less effective than listening and asking questions such that they come to their own solution or insight. This is the fundamental reason why coaching is predominantly a non-directive activity.

The word *authority* can give us an insight here. It has the same Latin root as the word *author*: a writer, someone who creates. The root is *auctum* which means, amongst other things, to produce, to increase, to cause to grow (*Shorter Oxford Dictionary on Historical Principles*). An author writes his own book. A manager dictating the book to be written would soon wear the patience of the writer, turning them into a mere scribe, thus destroying their motivation and in time their very ability to be creative.

In the past the failure to distinguish between the managing and the coaching elements has caused a kind of leakage. Line-managers try to handle performance and learning with a management style, command and control, rather than a more facilitative style. This derives from the fact that for most people those whom they have encountered who have been charged with helping them perform or learn effectively have also had a management responsibility. Teachers teach but they also ensure discipline in the class and at certain times pass judgement on their pupils' efforts, judgements that dictate the immediate future. This is true for line-managers too. And for the most part neither professional has recognised that the style appropriate to the one works less well for the other. One leaks into the other. The umpire and the coach in the tennis analogy have it easier as the role is split between them while the line-manager has to 'wear both hats'. There is a school of thought that proposes 'managing with a coaching style'. There have also been many articles with titles that are variations of 'The manager as coach'. This is another form of leakage. In one company that I know of it is almost impossible for a line-manager to give a direct instruction to a member of staff; they have to coach. I think this is just clumsy or incomplete thinking and can have the effect of undermining the line-manager and, ultimately, coaching itself. It is important to separate the circles one from the other.

Interestingly, when we distinguish both sides of the vertical line the management element takes up less time; as you place authority where it mostly belongs – with the player – the need to manage diminishes. It does not go away, but it takes less time. There is, it seems, a somewhat worrying corollary of this. Some years ago I ran a workshop for the UK management team of a well-known fast food chain with the intent of introducing them to coaching. The workshop was difficult; there was polite engagement but no passion, which is unusual. It was only afterwards when I reflected back on the event that I saw what had happened. You see, from their perspective there is only one way to cook a burger and quality (if that is what you call it) and consistency are everything. The shop-floor culture, one of managing, not coaching, had engulfed the leadership team. Clearly, if there is little or no need to coach then there should be little or no coaching; in some jobs standardisation is key to success. The problem here was that the leadership style had become very directive, resulting in a culture where risk was avoided and innovation suppressed. It is difficult for such a business to diversify.

These ideas about authority also relate to the third circle, leadership, where the line down the middle retains its validity. Sometimes it will be appropriate for a leader to make a clear and unequivocal statement about a direction to take, or to take a difficult decision without referring to others. At other times they may adopt a more facilitative, coaching, approach to a leadership issue and elicit a decision from others.

In summary let me suggest that there are a number of issues to be borne in mind for a line-manager:

- Line-managers need to manage and have a responsibility to both the employee and the organisation to do so.
- Line-managers, as part of managing, need to agree clear goals for their direct reports (*What*). Interestingly, while this is clearly a management task, using coaching skills to identify the goals in the first case is always more effective.
- Line-managers need to hold their direct reports to account for the goals that have been agreed.
- Once the goals have been agreed, and any other parameters surrounding their role such as values and behaviours, the line-manager coaches the direct report to achieve the agreed goals (*How*).
- Line-managers need to lead, to keep present in the minds of their direct reports the overarching aims of the organisation and be role-models for the desired values and behaviours.

I remind you of the ideas of flow in Chapter Four and you can see that line-management that embraces leadership, management and coaching can help create flow. Some of the conditions of flow are as follows:

- There are clear goals every step of the way.
- There is immediate feedback to one's actions.
- There is a balance between the challenges and the skills required.
- Action and awareness are merged.
- Distractions are excluded from consciousness.
- There is no worry of failure.
- Self-consciousness disappears.
- The activity becomes autotelic.

If you are reading this book from the perspective of a professional coach then you need to understand these guidelines and ensure that, if it is relevant to the objectives agreed with the player, they also understand these issues. The notion of authority in organisations is also important for the professional coach. The coach needs to understand that it is the organisation that is the client and therefore has a right and responsibility to influence the goals for any coaching intervention. The coaching itself, which will focus mostly on how to achieve the goals, is in the authority of the player and thus remains confidential. I will come back to this issue with more detail in the next chapter.

Having described at some length the place of coaching in the line-manager's role in a relatively theoretical manner, it is time to get practical again and to describe in detail how to apply it.

COACHING OPPORTUNITIES

The skills involved in coaching can be applied in many different ways and in many different environments, from the workplace to the schoolroom to the sports fields. As you internalise the skills and make them your own you will find that they show up in many aspects of your life. One of the exciting things about The School of Coaching is watching the participants progress through the programme and report at the various workshops how what they have learned has shown up in all areas of their lives: the consultant who was having a difficult meeting with a client and who was inspired to change the meeting into a coaching session; the Director of Training who found herself listening to her husband; the Senior Executive who began acknowledging the real talent and creativity his teenage daughter possessed. For me these are some of the more inspiring stories, not because they are so important and meaningful – which they are – but because it is a real demonstration that something has changed at a very fundamental level in the participants. These stories signal a shift from an earlier approach that was founded in the need to be in control, to be right, to fix, to heal, to make better (pick any one) to an approach that acknowledges the extraordinary capacity of human beings in which the primary skill is simply removing interference.

This, however, is a book about coaching in the workplace and there are obvious applications for the skills which is useful to examine. In the next few sections I want to give you some pictures of how a line-manager might use coaching skills.

Some coaching happens in a rather formal fashion. There is a clear and explicit agreement to coach between the coach and the player and it typically happens off-line, outside normal work activities. Coaching also takes place in a more informal way as part of the general run of play. It happens between colleagues at all levels in the organisation, between peers, between a line-manager and direct reports. It does not respect hierarchy; I remember asking a former boss just before a critical meeting what his ideal outcome from the meeting was. One successful meeting later he acknowledged the value of the question and how it had helped us retain focus in the meeting. Informal coaching does not necessarily require a clear agreement between coach and player (although most relationships work better when the parties know what is expected of them). Informal coaching happens on the spur of the moment. In the canteen a colleague indicates that he is having a difficult time with a particular client or with some aspect of a project. A member of staff complains that they will never get the job done on time. Both of these are opportunities for coaching. The conversation described in the opening chapter was just such an opportunity, one that could have been missed, and that Henry dismissed with 'It's bound to get better.' The possibilities for increased performance, for learning and for innovation that have been lost in this way are beyond number. At The School of Coaching in some workshops we get the participants to pair up and to give three-minute coaching sessions. They are always surprised at how much can be achieved in such a short space of time. This three-minute exercise was developed with a client in the USA, an international strategic management consultancy, where the only coaching you got from your partner occurred as you held the door of the taxi open for them. It became known as 'kerbside coaching'. At the School we have re-named it 'corridor coaching' partly because that would seem to present more opportunities (not subject to the weather) and partly because of the desire not to be associated with other kerbside professions.

It is in situations such as these that the line-manager who coaches shows up most clearly and can have a profound and lasting effect on the performance and learning of his direct reports. And frankly it is a significantly more rewarding way of doing business. When this happens an organisation truly has a 'coaching culture'. As the Human Resource Director of an international beverage producer and distributor observed, 'This is not about Innovation with a capital "I" in our business but rather about hundreds and hundreds of innovations, small "i", all across the organisation, in every conversation.'

The remainder of this chapter discusses some of the principal applications, again presented from a line-manager's perspective.

Line-manager coaching direct reports

The most obvious of all applications in the workplace is that of a line-manager coaching those who report to him or her, whether in the formal or informal sense. This book and in particular this chapter is a plea to take the coaching element more seriously so that the player performs more effectively, learns and get some fulfilment. As I said earlier, coaching where there is a line-management relationship presents some difficulties in that the line-manager has power in the face of which it can be awkward to create an environment of trust. Another difficulty is that the player may simply want to be directed, and may not want to have to think for himself and to take responsibility. These difficulties are not insurmountable and some of them are addressed in the section headed 'Obstacles and pitfalls for the line-manager' in the following chapter.

Coaching in the management processes

Most organisations have a number of management processes that lend themselves to coaching, in particular the people-management processes such as performance reviews, appraisals, development reviews, objective setting meetings and progress reviews. It staggers me that in this day and age there are still organisations where the line-manager sets the subordinate's goals. I can think of few quicker, more sure-fire ways to erode motivation and undermine responsibility. Most organisations are more enlightened than that and allow for self-assessment on the part of the subordinate and for them to identify their own goals. Both of these are perfect opportunities to wrap coaching around management processes. Think about the really critical conversations, the ones that have significant impact in organisations, for example conversations to set objectives, to agree budgets, to establish or review projects. Imagine if these conversations were 'redesigned' as coaching conversations. Take the budgeting process. The direct report is sent off to prepare a budget. After a while they come back with their best effort and are told to strip out ten percent of the costs, and what about the new product launch? So there's another iteration and probably another. In this process time is wasted, enthusiasm eroded and the relationship between line-manager and direct report undermined. And there is little or no learning. With effective coaching these consequences would be less likely to accrue, a great boost to organisational effectiveness.

Coaching during major change

One of the debilitating side-effects of major change, be it organisational or cultural, is fear and uncertainty. This results in large numbers of people looking for answers to an array of questions, usually from the leadership group. Adopting a coaching approach has a number of benefits. First, it has the effect of putting ownership and control back into the hands of the player and this can lessen anxiety. Secondly, in change situations where there are often no right answers, coaching will draw out possibilities and options from which the best can be selected. Thirdly, it gives some respite to the leaders as others begin to take responsibility and join in the game. Leaders can't, and shouldn't, do it all.

Before and after training events

Coaching can be used to great effect to ensure that someone gets full value from a training programme. The manager or trainer can coach a delegate prior to the event so that he is very clear about his learning objectives. When the event is completed a further coaching session can consolidate the learning and ensure that it gets applied in the workplace to best effect. There is evidence that suggests that the effectiveness of training can be increased by the order of twenty-five percent in this way.

Coaching as part of leadership

Effective leadership is so dependent on the personality of the leader and the followers, the culture of the organisation and the nature of the business that I am not going to be foolish and make a statement about good leadership. What I will say is that when there is an alignment between what inspires an individual, the job they are doing and the direction of the company, then people at all levels can give of their best freely, communication becomes easier and phenomenal results accrue. A coaching approach, that directly involves staff in the direction the business is taking and the shape of their job, can be part of what creates that alignment.

Coaching can also be used to gain buy-in to organisational values and behaviours. For instance, working with a player to identify her own values and then helping her relate these to the organisation's values and finding those elements that are congruent, and those that are not, will bring the values to life in a meaningful way, particularly if there is room for debate – and influencing – around those elements where there is discomfort.

Coaching on projects

Coaching is a great way to go about delivering projects within time and within budget. It is very similar to coaching teams (Chapter 10) and so I refer you to that chapter.

Coaching upwards

'Is it possible to coach my boss?' is a question frequently asked at coaching skills workshops. The answer is that anyone can be coached – if they are willing. What is interesting, I think, is what is behind the question. This is usually a different question: 'How can I change my boss's behaviour?' To this question there is a different answer: you cannot change anyone else's behaviour, only they can. What you can do is give them some feedback. If they are willing to hear the feedback and understand it then coaching may be appropriate. After that they have the right to choose their coach, which may or may not be the person giving the feedback. In my experience it is unusual for a boss to be willing to be coached by a subordinate, but not unheard of. When it does happen it is a tremendously powerful signal that the boss is truly open to learning and meaningful communication, the impact of which extends well beyond the person who volunteered the feedback in the first place. This scenario fits into my loose definition of formal coaching. Coaching upwards in the informal sense can happen much more easily and frequently but is dependent on the prevailing culture in the organisation and on just how much a control junky – or how desperate – the person 'upwards' of you is.

Coaching peers

Coaching between friends and within a peer group is perhaps the easiest environment in which to coach in the sense that there are the fewest obstacles to an effective relationship. This is because it is less likely than in a line relationship that there are competing agendas or that the coach has an investment in the outcome (other than that the session should be successful, which is an obstacle in itself).

Some organisations have instituted a system of 'buddy' coaching or co-coaching. The notion here is that two people who have some training in coaching skills support each other in the pursuit of performance or learning objectives. As you might imagine, some of the pairings meet once or twice and then the pressures of work override the initial good intentions. Other pairings maintain the practice even when the individuals move on to other parts of the business or to other countries, resorting to the phone for their coaching fix. I know of at least one case where the buddy coaching relationship has persisted after both protagonists have moved to new companies.

Mentoring

In principle, mentoring is concerned with longer-term career issues, while coaching is more concerned with more immediate performance issues. The point to be made here is that the models, tools and skills that are critical to coaching as I have described them will also make a more effective mentor. A mentor who is reliant on, say, an avuncular style and dependent on having had significant experience of the organisation, business and life may well provide great benefit and be a wonderful person to be with. However, at the very least such a mentor would need to be able to listen effectively in order to ensure that the pearls of wisdom were indeed pearls in the eyes of the recipient. On a more positive note a mentor who has vast experience, and can use it to good effect, and who can also employ a non-directive approach when appropriate will have much greater impact.

Outside the workplace there are many other opportunities to use coaching.

Coaching your partner

'Don't do your professional stuff on me.' I have heard those words a few times, not without justification, for coaching a partner can seem intrusive and patronising. Effective coaching requires that there is a relationship in which the coach can divorce (there's a joke there somewhere) himself or herself from the outcome and from what is going on for the player. In a relationship in which two people have a commitment to each other and whose lives have become entwined, such a separation is often difficult and sometimes virtually impossible. However, acknowledging that there are some quite tough obstacles to the use of coaching within say, a marital relationship, it is not impossible and may even be a sign of a healthy and mature relationship. The key is to identify and talk about the obstacles before doing any coaching.

Coaching children

Coaching other people's children is almost the easiest of all applications and the most fun. In my relationship with my stepdaughter, Victoria, my coaching skills have played an important part, particularly when it comes to homework, as I have already indicated with the 'overdue essay' story (Chapter 4). In general terms, when she gets stuck with something the truth is that she probably knows more about the topic than I, so helping her think it through is the most valuable assistance I can give. (I also happen to believe that homework is for her to do and not me, so if I use coaching she gets

to write her own essay and use her own prolific imagination.)
Coaching and all the skills involved have a wonderful place in the
relationship with children. In the teenage years, where nothing
seems to work, the least you can do is listen. I will not pretend to
have been always successful in this domain.

Coaching yourself

In a sense you are coaching yourself all the time. When you take
your nose out of this book to ponder some point, be it a new insight
or a disagreement you have with something that I have written, one
could argue that you are coaching yourself. When you take time out
to consider a project you are engaged in or ask yourself 'Hold on,
how do I really want this to be?' you are coaching yourself. Some of
the most valuable time that I spend on behalf on my own clients is
when I take the dog for a walk – I just have not yet found a way of
charging for it, although I guess I could set the dog's expenses
against my tax bill. However, there are limitations to a person's ability to coach himself or herself. Coaching is about raising awareness.
If I consider an issue on my own and in isolation at a certain level I
will be trapped by my own patterns of thought. From the inside I
cannot see me. Part of why coaching works is because, in that
moment when the player communicates to another and is understood, the thoughts are externalised and a certain distance is
achieved between the player and their thoughts and emotions. If
you recall the analogy of the man in his car in the traffic jam
(Chapter 6), he is now on the bus, upstairs on the front seat, just
noticing.

There are some techniques that you can use to externalise your
thoughts and achieve some objectivity. For instance, a former colleague tells the story of an argument he had with his wife. At some
point, in desperation, he left the house, as he tells it letting the front
door do the talking. Once outside on the pavement he brought his

breathing into focus and relaxed somewhat. He then proceeded to coach himself. Inspired, this is what he did. He walked first on the left-hand side of the pavement and from this position, this physical place, he was coach and asked questions. Having asked the question he then moved to the right-hand side of the pavement from which place, as player, he answered the questions. While this was difficult for other pavement users and upsetting for the neighbours who must have thought him to be drunk as he weaved his way around the block, my colleague did get to some resolution. Another technique which works quite well is to write your thoughts down on paper, using the GROW model to structure the ideas.

Opportunities to coach are all around us. I suggest you start by simply noticing them and then, when you have the right permissions, take them: they are opportunities for achievement, fulfilment and joy.

Chapter 9
Getting started

Learning the skills of coaching is a relatively easy task and in a workshop situation most people can achieve a level of skill in a few days. The problems arise when they get back to their places of work, where business, the prevailing culture and the expectations of co-workers, the boss and direct reports, tend to undermine the good intentions expressed at the end of the workshop. In this sense then this is the most important part of the book. Of course the skills are important but I suggest that even a relatively unskilled coach whose heart is in the right place is a lot better than someone who gives no coaching at all. Now that I think of it, I am not sure it is possible to be a 'bad' coach if your heart is in the right place; a solid 'inner game' spawns a solid 'outer game'.

This chapter comes in three parts. The first is intended to show how a line-manager might introduce coaching to their (as yet) unsuspecting direct reports; the second covers the same ground but for the professional coach. The third part is relevant to both line-manager and coach as it looks at building an effective coaching relationship and at setting goals. I debated with myself where to put the section on goal setting. I have decided to put it in this chapter because it is so fundamental to the relationship (without a clear purpose the relationship falls apart) and because a clear focus is such a crucial element of effective coaching in the workplace.

GETTING STARTED AS A LINE-MANAGER

The following options are not the only ways of starting to coach direct reports; they are simply some methods tried and tested by participants on the programmes at the School. Many of them can be used together. I am slightly concerned that this section will seem repetitive of those elements of the previous chapter that describe where coaching fits in the line-manager's role. The intent here is different from that in Chapter 8; it is to suggest how specifically one might begin.

Through the appraisal or performance review

The obvious place to begin coaching is in the appraisal or performance review. Not only will the line-manager use coaching skills to define and agree objectives and success measures, but also the outcomes from such events will include a set of objectives for the player to pursue, most of which will be suitable topics for coaching. The foundation for on-going coaching is thus set and continues in the monthly one-on-ones. In addition many people I have worked with have an item on the agenda of their monthly one-on-ones with their direct reports that is entirely at the discretion of the direct report. As trust builds, underlying issues that impact on performance are often brought up, such as self-confidence or relationships. You may have gleaned from this that I believe it is a matter of not just 'best practice' but of critical importance to have regular one-on-ones between a line-manager and a direct report. This method has an advantage over many other ways of introducing coaching in that the prospective player will have experienced coaching already in the meeting and will have some sense of what they are letting themself in for.

Using feedback as the starting point

This is another easy and uncomplicated way of bringing coaching into the workplace. To introduce coaching in this way requires that there is some real feedback to be given and that it is substantive, by which I mean that it is not something the receiver of the feedback can change simply and immediately. Assuming those two requirements are in place, when the line-manager has successfully given the feedback they then offer support in the form of coaching. If the coaching is seen to work, it is a relatively simple task to introduce other topics onto the agenda and thus establish an on-going coaching agenda. The feedback can be given as part of a regular series of one-on-one meetings or might arise from a specific event. In either case the line-manager is indicating that a change is required and is offering to support the direct report in making the desired change. I refer you back to Chapter 7 and the section on giving feedback for additional information.

Through a team agreement

This is a very powerful way to introduce coaching because it involves making explicit agreements in public that are thereafter more difficult to ignore or forget. It assumes that the line-manager has a team of people reporting directly, and involves bringing the team together for a meeting that, at a minimum, would have the following outcomes:

- A collective understanding of what coaching is, including the notions of non-directive coaching and formal and informal coaching
- Agreement about how and when coaching will be used
- The ground rules for coaching. This should include an agreement about confidentiality and may also include discussion

about how topics get onto the coaching agenda, timing and frequency of one-on-one meetings, formal and/or informal coaching and how to give feedback.

It is a good idea to demonstrate coaching during the meeting with a willing team member, as this is the most direct way of communicating what coaching is. The volunteer player must choose a real topic to be coached on, otherwise the demonstration will not work. The beauty of this approach is that it allows for open discussion about the effectiveness of the coaching approach and the line-manager's proficiency. There are two additions to this approach:

- The meeting can be facilitated by an external coach, which allows the line-manager to participate fully.
- The meeting, and subsequent follow-up meetings, can start with giving feedback to the line-manager on their coaching.

The following are possible agenda items for such a meeting:

- Describe the purpose of the meeting and the desired outcomes. A coach would also ask if there were any other outcomes the group wanted.
- Define coaching. A good approach is to get the team to share their individual experiences of effective and ineffective coaching, whether that coaching took place in work, in sport or in school or university. The definition of coaching given earlier might also help.
- Demonstrate a coaching session. First describe the GROW model and then demonstrate with a willing volunteer. It is a good idea to identify the volunteer beforehand and to make sure that they have a real issue to be coached on. Set a time limit for the session: 20 minutes is about as much as spectators can manage. After the session, review it in the group.

- Discuss with the team what the applications of coaching might be. Out of all the possible applications agree with the team the ones that are appropriate and how the team might get started.
- Ask what ground rules would help in making the coaching effective. Make sure that the issues of confidentiality and feedback to the line-manager get discussed.

Through an individual agreement

It follows, of course, that pretty much the same approach that I have described for introducing coaching via teams can be used on a one-on-one basis. It implies a fairly formal coaching relationship. This would work well with someone whose performance is poor or equally someone with very stretching goals. The initial meeting in the coaching programme outlined later in this chapter describes how to get one-on-one coaching started in detail.

Alongside tasks, projects or change programmes

Introducing coaching in order to assist individuals or teams achieve important tasks or projects or to see through the delivery of a change initiative is arguably the most successful route to implementing coaching. It makes it clear that coaching is not some new trend in the organisation. Rather it puts coaching in its proper context – performance and learning. At the time when the individual or the team is being offered the new task the line-manager can offer coaching support.

OBSTACLES AND PITFALLS FOR THE LINE-MANAGER

As an activity coaching is really rather simple. That does not mean that coaching is easy. With a little bit of discipline most people can learn to listen and the GROW model is hardly rocket science. The difficulties, such as they are, often lie outside the skills. Here are two prime examples of obstacles and pitfalls that line-managers may have to face in trying to establish an effective coaching relationship.

When the direct report does not want to be coached

The first rule is that if someone does not want to be coached then attempting to coach will get you nowhere. If an individual in a work organisation is achieving all their goals, is not disrupting things for others and does not want to be coached, then leave them alone. If, on the other hand, they are not achieving their goals and they refuse coaching then the line-manager needs to be really clear that this is no longer a coaching issue and has become a management issue. Most organisations have a well-established process for handling these situations that is the province of the Human Resource department.

When openness and judgement clash

Many years ago I had a conversation with my then line-manager about my sales performance. The performance itself was not the issue, although it could have been better; it was that I hated making cold calls to prospective clients. We had a brief conversation about this that I took to be coaching. Some six months afterwards at the annual performance review I made my case for an increase in salary and for promotion. This was rejected because, by my own admission, I was not good at selling. As I pointed out earlier the line-manager wears two hats; one (managing) requires making judgements about another's performance that has significant impact on that other's pay and prospects, while wearing the other hat (coaching) requires them to create an environment where the player, the direct report, can be open and vulnerable. Incompatible you might think. Maybe not. I suggested earlier that it was difficult to coach one's partner. I suggested this once at a workshop and was picked up by a participant. 'Not impossible – there's just a lot of interference' was the response. The ability both to coach and manage another requires a strong, honest relationship where there are clear performance goals and success measures, thus bringing as much objectivity as possible to the assessment of performance. Both these issues are addressed in more detail at the end of this chapter.

GETTING STARTED AS A PROFESSIONAL COACH

This section is not about how to establish yourself as a professional coach. That's another book and there are people better qualified than me to write it. It is about how a professional coach, whether an external or internal agent, delivers value over time to the player and the client, i.e. the organisation in which they work. My approach to this is to describe a coaching programme. In doing this I am indicating a formal relationship that takes place over a period of time and that is designed to help the player achieve substantial goals. Such a programme has a number of elements that I will describe in some detail. Not all these elements will be appropriate for every situation, so this is really a pick-and-mix affair. To tell the truth I have probably never run a coaching programme that included all the elements described. What actually occurs is a far more fluid and natural process. But all the elements have their place and I believe it is therefore important to understand each of them, not least because they collectively represent a wonderful checklist (Diagram 9).

Initial meeting

Purpose: To establish whether there is a need for coaching, achieve agreement in principle, build relationship and establish the ground rules.

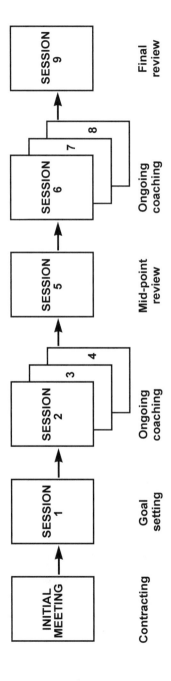

Diagram 9. Outline of a typical coaching programme.

1 Formal introductions achieved, the coach suggests the above as the purpose of the meeting.

2 An easy starting point is the player's background. This might include an overview of the educational and professional history and a description of their current role.

3 The next talking point is probably about the reasons why coaching is on the cards, what prompted the introduction and what the player is hoping to achieve through coaching.

4 The conversation then shifts to what coaching is, possibly introducing the GROW model, the spectrum of coaching styles and a description of a typical programme.

5 At this point there will be an emerging sense that coaching is either the right way to go, or not. If not, have the courage to say so and support the player in finding what they need.

6 If it does seem appropriate, then a discussion about the ground rules for the programme is next on the agenda. Issues to cover here include confidentiality, honesty, openness, feedback to the coach, and logistical issues such as venue, duration of programme and sessions and postponement of sessions (hours notice, etc.).

7 Seek a commitment to go ahead. Remember you have to make a commitment too, and that you need to feel confident in your ability to deliver on your part of the bargain. If you are not confident try to identify the obstacle and address it – if appropriate – with the player.

8 With agreement to proceed in place, the coach should talk through the first session (outlined below) to identify any materials or information that is required for the session.

9 If the client for the programme (he who pays the bills or has commissioned the coach) is not the player, the coach and player should discuss how the client is to be kept informed (see 'Public and private goals' later in this chapter). It is always best that the

player is responsible for this, thus protecting the trust in the relationship.

Session One: Establishing context and programme goals

Purpose: To identify and agree specific goals and success measures for the programme such that the needs of the player and the client are met.

1 The coach declares the purpose of the session and asks the player if they have any additional goals.

2 Given that the player's needs do not change the nature of the session, the coach starts by asking the player what their goals are for the coaching programme. This may duplicate part of the initial meeting, in which case check that the goals have not changed. Then bring into the discussion the various sources from which goals might emerge:

- The client's perception (e.g. the HR Manager)
- The player's manager's perception
- Feedback to the player
- The player's current business objectives
- The player's career vision
- Recent appraisals, performance reviews or personal development plans
- Strategic initiatives and change programmes in the organisation.

All of the above may inform the player's goals. The feedback to the player can come from sources such as any existing 360° survey, interviews conducted with the player's direct reports and the line-manager.

3   The next step is to identify the success measures for the pro-
    gramme. I suggest how to do this towards the end of this chap-
    ter.

4   If there is a requirement to keep a third party informed, such as
    the client or the player's line-manager, then sending a copy of
    the goals to that individual for agreement and input is an appro-
    priate step. It may be that there will be a set of public goals and
    one or two private goals shared only between the coach and the
    player, where the issues are of a more personal nature. This is a
    legitimate practice as long as the coach and player are agreed that
    the achievement of the private goals contributes towards the
    player's productivity in the client organisation.

5   The final step might be to check that the goals identified are
    achievable in the time frame of the programme and in the num-
    ber of sessions contracted.

Session Two and subsequent sessions

Purpose: To make progress towards the programme goals.

1   The coach declares the purpose of the session – in words less for-
    mal than those above – and asks the player what they want to
    achieve in the session. While a principle of coaching is 'following
    interest' it is important that the topic(s) for the session are con-
    sidered in relation to the goals for the overall programme. It is
    often all too compelling for the player to choose a topic that is,
    literally, the last thing on their mind – a recent insight or upset –
    and not deal with the issues that will take them towards their
    longer-term goals.

2   With the topics for the session agreed, the actions from the pre-
    vious meeting are reviewed.

3   That done, each of the identified topics is worked through using
    the GROW model.

4   The penultimate step in the session is to pull together the action plan.

5   The final step in any session is to request feedback from the player. This is important not just for the learning of the coach but because it demonstrates a commitment to openness, builds trust and develops the relationship, making it possible for the player in turn to be open and trusting.

Mid-programme review

Purpose: To check progress towards the programme goals and review the coaching relationship. Ideally the mid-term review will form the first part of a typical session, leaving time for some coaching in the meeting.

1   Progress towards the programme goals is reviewed, the ground rules are reviewed, the effectiveness of the coaching is discussed and feedback from the player is solicited. Sometimes players are reluctant to give feedback, often because they do not want to upset the coach and run the risk of damaging an important relationship. In order to move beyond this, I find that if I reflect on the sessions before the meeting then I can usually identify a number of issues that I am not comfortable with in my own performance. If the player is not forthcoming with feedback then I can ask specific questions and this will break the deadlock. On a longer programme it may be appropriate to seek feedback on the player's progress from other parties such as the client, their manager, their direct reports and other colleagues or peers.

2   Time permitting, other topics are identified and worked through and the action plan agreed.

Final review and completion

Purpose: To assess progress towards the programme goals and complete the relationship.

In the final session it is important to take the time to review the programme. This allows both the player and the coach to maximise their learning from the event and to complete the relationship. Relationships that are incomplete, that drift into separation, retain some of the emotional energy that was invested in them. This energy is not available for other relationships or activities. For instance, if the player cancels a session and then, for reasons of business or whatever, the session is not re-booked, the coach may spend a considerable amount of energy wondering what went wrong or whether he was doing a good job. It might even undermine his confidence. The player on the other hand may be embarrassed or feeling guilty and spend time worrying what he is going to say when he meets up with the coach. The outline for the session is similar to the mid-programme review as outlined before. If the client and the player are different people then the client should be included in the process of completion. The coaching may end at this point or a different relationship may emerge, such as quarterly meetings, in which case return to square one and start off the programme again as outlined above. I like to finish coaching relationships by helping the player to identify the specific things that they have learned during the course of the coaching relationship, as it is typically these lessons that are the legacy from the coaching, rather then the goals achieved, and works against dependency, on the part of the player, on the coach.

The contract

It is useful to have a clear, written contract with the player. There is also a need to have a contract with the client – the organisation –

and this is best expressed in the public and private goals matrix (as described at the end of this chapter). One does not want to be too heavy-handed with this and present it as if it were a legal document or for either party to feel constrained by it. The purpose of the contract is to ensure an effective, hassle-free relationship and, like any contract, you do not need it until you do. At which point if you do not have one it is too late. It should include the programme goals and success measures, the ground rules and if appropriate the fees.

Meeting duration and frequency

There are no set rules about the frequency and duration of meetings and each coaching relationship will develop its own pattern. The place to start, as you might guess, is by asking the player. Additionally there are some factors that should be considered in developing a programme:

- The time frame in which the goals are to be achieved
- The player's need for support
- The level of stretch in the goals.

I find it very difficult to get anything meaningful done, when coaching in the formal sense, in anything under an hour and will usually book a one-and-a-half or two-hour session. This is also driven by the fact that I am not on site in the way most managers are and I want to make sure that the sessions are complete. If the coach and player work in the same building it is easier to reconvene or catch up between meetings. At the beginning of a coaching relationship, meetings tend to happen more frequently, say fortnightly, and then change to a three-week or a monthly pattern. This is because players tend to need more support in the early stages as they consider making changes and begin to implement them.

Meeting Report

Name   David O'Hara
Organisation Network Bank plc
Coach   Myles Downey
Date   23/5/03
Meeting no.   6

Topics discussed
We reviewed the Actions from meeting 5. The only outstanding action was the conversation with Gerry to clarify the purpose and parameters for the Axis project.

We also reviewed the overall goals for the programme. The only major change we agreed was to change the priorities. You felt that the performance – and support of – your direct reports had become more important as this should free you up to look to longer term matters.

The performance of your direct reports became the principal topic for the session. You identified 'three levers' that you have available to improve performance and give more support
- re-visiting each individual's performance goals so that there is greater clarity and that the priorities are agreed
- giving accurate feedback on performance to date (in the past you have tended to avoid potentially uncomfortable situations)
- re-establishing monthly meetings with the individuals and the team where there is a specific slot for your direct reports to bring up their issues

Finally, we spoke briefly about how you might approach the next executive meeting. You have been given feedback that you are seen as too confrontational by your peers. At the next meeting you will try two things
- being very clear about your intent in making any intervention and telling your peers what it is
- taking a little more time to understand each contributor; asking questions, etc.

Next actions
Hold meeting with Gerry.
Write and send an e-mail to your direct reports about how you intend to improve performance and increase support.
Get Tessa to book team and individual meetings for the next 6 months.

Next meeting
10th June, 8.30am at your offices.

Diagram 10. Meeting report.

Meeting reports

Meeting reports are documents that contain the vital information from a coaching session. At a minimum this should include the topics discussed, the key points and the actions arising from the discussion. There are two main schools of thought that I know of in relation to meeting reports. One school has it that the coach should write up the meeting, the other (not surprisingly) advocates that the player should. In both cases there is agreement that having a record of what was discussed and agreed, together with the action points, is a necessity. The argument for having the player write up the notes is that in the writing the player will achieve another level of clarity and responsibility. When the coach is external to the organisation, and providing a service, then perhaps the coach should complete the meeting report. I have taken to using a pre-printed sheet (Diagram 10) which I fill in before the end of the meeting and then photocopy, leaving a copy with the player and keeping one for my own records.

PRACTICE PLAYERS

There is another sense in which 'getting started' is important for the professional coach. Inevitably there is a moment before you are a professional coach; you are an apprentice or a novice. To build confidence and to iron out any flaws in your approach, one possibility is to adopt what we in The School of Coaching call 'practice players'. This is before the first paying client. People learn coaching most effectively when two factors are present; the player is addressing real issues (role-playing does not work as the player can keep on inventing new circumstances – there is no 'truth') and the learning environment is safe. That is to say that it takes the pressure to perform, to 'get it right', off the coach, and sets the scene for more relaxed coaching sessions in which the coach can get quality feedback from the player. Outside a workshop the best way to establish these factors is to work with practice players. Practice players are people with a real interest in being coached who understand that the coach is still in training. The notion of 'real interest' means that the person is committed to getting value from the coaching, not just engaging because they are a good person and want to support the novice coach. This is also a powerful way for a line-manager to introduce coaching while continuing to learn. Maybe all sessions should be viewed as 'practice sessions' by the coach because it removes the interference called 'this is important/serious' and in such an atmosphere of mutuality and playfulness both parties make the most progress. I notice that coaches often feel that they have to do it right and that they cannot make mistakes. What nonsense. As long as I have a strong relationship with the player I should feel free to try new things and get it wrong – all in the service of the player and the client. If I do get it wrong I just need to acknowledge it and try again.

OBSTACLES AND PITFALLS FOR THE PROFESSIONAL COACH

While the issues raised in this section are of particular importance to the professional coach they can also crop up for the line-manager.

When the player is seen to be failing

It is very difficult to coach successfully in a 'remedial' situation. And I use the word remedial very deliberately because that is often how organisations – or people in organisations - hold it when a staff member is seen to be failing. One of the reasons people fail in organisations is because the organisation has let them down. Of course I do not want to take the responsibility away from the individual, and if an individual is failing then they need to take responsibility for that and take some action. But in any relationship, and I include the relationship between a staff member and an organisation, there is one hundred percent responsibility for the relationship on both sides. I do know that that makes two hundred percent.

There are two reasons in particular to be cautious:

1 The organisation may have already rejected the player but has not admitted it. In this case, even if the coaching is successful, the organisation may be unable, or unwilling, to re-admit the player.
2 The player may have already rejected the organisation and again not admitted it.

I have frequently been called into situations by clients where the player is deemed to be failing. The problem is often that the player has not been given the feedback early enough - if at all - or that the line-manager has been unwilling to bite the bullet and have the difficult conversation. So they get the executive coach in to sort it out. The most useful thing that can be done in these situations is to get the manager, or the Human Resource department, to have a frank conversation with the 'failing' employee so that all parties know where they stand. After that, coaching may be possible but I would want everyone to know that a possible outcome from the coaching would be that the player might decide to leave the organisation.

Who is the client?

Whether you are an external executive coach or a manager, when you engage in coaching you need to be very clear as to who the client is. Many people, particularly external coaches with a background in the psychological professions – where confidentiality is all – believe it to be the person they are coaching. It may sometimes be the case that the player and the client are the same person but mostly they are separate. The client is the organisation or its representative, the person paying the bill. And the client has rights too – the right to make an input to the goals of the coaching so that the player can deliver in line with the organisation's needs. This problem is in part resolved by the use of the public/private goals matrix at the end of this chapter, in part by the coach's capacity to understand the organisation's need and in part by the integrity of the coach and the player.

It's not therapy

Sometimes it seems to me that a good listener creates a vacuum, a silence, which others feel compelled to fill. And as the speaker notices that what they are saying is not being evaluated or judged they begin to trust. So they say some more, they say things that they would never dream of saying under other circumstances. The things that taxi drivers have said to me when all I have been doing is sitting quietly in the back seat of their cab, listening but not judging, are beyond belief and, in some cases, repetition. It happens occasionally in coaching sessions that the player broaches a topic – because they trust the coach – that may well be better handled by a counsellor or therapist. If this happens the coach should abandon coaching, but – please – not listening, and refer the player to a counsellor or therapist.

THE COACHING RELATIONSHIP

Effective coaching rests on a solid relationship between coach and player. It seems such an obvious thing, too obvious to have to write it down, but the truth is that the only thing that can cause coaching to fail is an insufficiently strong relationship. As a practising coach and a supervisor of other people's development as coaches, I notice that almost every unsuccessful coaching intervention is the result of a ropey relationship.

In Chapter 5 in the skills matrix I refer to the skill set of 'building relationship' and describe the intent as being 'to create an environment in which the player feels safe and unjudged'. Without a relationship there is no coaching. In fact the only real mistake that a coach can make is to damage the relationship irreparably. Everything else is recoverable. Coaching fails when something is left unsaid, or even when the player feels they have to leave something unsaid. The relationship has to be sufficiently strong for the player to trust in the coach. The player has to feel safe to say whatever is on their mind, to own up to mistakes and weaknesses, to suggest the absurd or the impossible: in a word, to be vulnerable. The player must feel free to challenge the coach and to give feedback, to say 'this isn't working' or 'I don't understand the question' or 'no, I don't want to consider that option yet – this one is more interesting'. I want you to be clear that to have a good coaching relationship does not necessarily mean that you have to like the player. Sure, it helps if the two of you are going to be locked away in a room together for an hour or more, but that is not what does it. Care does it and I can care for someone that I do not like.

The practical, mechanistic aspects of establishing a good coaching relationship have been dealt with earlier in this chapter. Here I would like to discuss what underpins that relationship. As you will see, all the relationship foundations are manifestations of caring. A willingness to listen and understand are also core elements. The qualities of a good coaching relationship include the following.

Trust

The player needs to be able to trust fully in the coach. They need to trust that whatever they say will not be repeated to anyone else, to trust that their thoughts, beliefs, fears and ideas will be respected and not ridiculed, to trust in the coach's intention to be of real assistance. And to trust that the information elicited in the session will not be divulged to others.

Equally the coach needs to be able to trust in the player. To trust that the player is fully engaged in getting value, to trust that they are being as truthful as is possible. I have occasionally found myself in a coaching relationship where the player was participating because it would look good to their superiors; that they were in some sense demonstrating a willingness to change when this was far from the truth. As soon as I detect this I will gracefully confront the player. Two things tend to happen at this point. Sometimes the coaching ends there and then but with the relationship intact (OK, almost), or the individual chooses to engage for real.

Honesty

The player needs to be honest in telling it as they really see it or believe it to be, in taking responsibility for their actions, perceptions and beliefs. And the coach needs to be honest with the player. This is a more difficult one because a player will occasionally ask for the coach's opinion – and the opinion is likely to include some judgement or assessment. Judgement and assessment do not fit easily with a non-judgemental, non-directive coaching style. And yet there is a need to be honest. So if the coach is asked for an opinion the first thing to do is to find out why the player requires the opinion. Very often asking the question 'For what reason do you want my opinion?' will allow the player to see that they were looking for reassurance, and once that has been understood they may no longer require the coach's opinion. Another tack is to turn the request back to the player as in 'I'll give you my opinion if you want it, but before I do, tell me what your own point of view is.' If, after both of these questions, the player still wants the coach's opinion then he might choose to give it. I am usually quite willing to express a point of view on a plan of action, an idea or behaviour. I would resist responding to a question such as 'What do you think of me?' and challenge why the player wanted to know. After all, it is just my 'stuff', my judgements, and has no real validity or currency.

Openness

Openness is obviously critical in the coaching relationship. And coaches need to recognise that this is the most hard-earned factor in relationship building, even more so than honesty. Coaching requires *complete* honesty, but only *appropriate* openness. So there is a judgement call to be made. Appropriate means that all the information that the player possesses, all the thoughts, ideas and beliefs that are needed to make progress on the topic, are available and part of the discussion. Other things, however, need not enter into the sessions if they are not needed to make progress. It is likely that the player will have thoughts, ideas and beliefs that they would never reveal to anyone, let alone a work colleague, or they may simply have promised confidentiality on an issue. If a situation arises in which the player is unable to be open, and this is explicit, i.e. they are honest about it, then that in itself is a sign of a healthy relationship. They just may need to find another coach – or a counsellor – for that particular topic.

Transparency/intent

We touched on this already in Chapter 7 in the context of proposing effectively. Transparency means that one's intentions, within the context of the coaching, are completely clear to the other party and, almost certainly, explicitly so. Transparency is a quick way to build trust in a relationship. As a relationship develops there is typically less need for it to be present explicitly, because the partners trust each other's good intentions. Transparency in a coaching session, coming from the coach, sounds like

'My intention in giving you this feedback is to broaden your understanding.'

'I really did not understand what you just said. Can you say it again?'

'I need to understand this part better. Can you tell me about it?'

'I am really sorry, I lost concentration …'

'I'd like you to try this visioning exercise. I believe it will help clarify what you really want.'

'I have a suggestion for you. Do you want it?'

In the name of transparency I introduce new clients to the GROW model and the spectrum of coaching styles in the first meeting so that they know what I am doing in the session. To better understand the importance of transparency, just think how not understanding the coach's intentions would impact on the player. I suggest that they'd find it difficult to trust the coach, to be honest and appropriately open. No coaching.

SETTING GOALS AND DEFINING SUCCESS CRITERIA

This section could reasonably have been included in Chapter 7, 'Proposing'. But because the quality of the goals and success measures that are agreed at the beginning of a coaching programme is the single greatest factor – after the relationship – that impacts on the success of the coaching, it seems to me to fit well in the present chapter, 'Getting Started'.

Setting goals

Many readers will be familiar with the SMART acronym. This suggests that goals should be specific, measurable, achievable, realistic and in a clear time frame. These are useful guidelines and all goals should be measured against them. Here I want to talk about different types of goals and to link them on a matrix (Diagram 11).

The matrix has three main vertical columns. The middle column (which is from where I mostly commence my coaching sessions) is for performance goals. These describe what the player is seeking to achieve during the course of the coaching programme or the term of the coaching (i.e. a year where the line-manager is the coach). A professional coach will draw on the annual goals that the player has agreed with the line-manager to start off this column. The column on the left is for learning or development goals. I will often find the content for this column by asking: 'In order to achieve your performance goals, what do you need to learn?'. Another question that is useful here is this: 'In order for you to achieve your longer-term goals or vision what do you need to learn?'.

The right-hand column is for success measures or specific behaviours that the player wants to adopt. Success measures, which I talk about next, relate directly to the performance goals, and the question might be: 'When you have successfully achieved your goal, how will you know?' New, desired behaviours can emerge of their own right, as a result of feedback or as a function of cultural change in the organisation. The matrix itself has some good examples. Clearly, you can start with any column, following the interest of the player.

Public and private goals

I have suggested that the client, the organisation – the payer of the bills and salaries – has some rights. They will need to know that the

PROGRAMME GOALS

Player	Coach	Start date	Completion date
Sean O'Driscoll	Myles Downey	3.10.03	3.4.04

	Learning goals	Performance goals	Success measures/behaviours
Public goals	To be able to write compelling proposals for $50,000 and over	To deliver $250,000 sales in the first half-year	Receipts totalling $250,000 filed Rewards to sales team for each sale of $50,000 and over
	To revisit recruitment skills notes	To build a 'sales machine' for the Southwest region capable of sales of at least $1.5m	Two new sales executives recruited Sales tracking system designed and installed on intranet
	To learn how to facilitate effective sales team meetings (keeping the focus on results)	To build a strong sales and sales support team	Information shared No divide between backroom and sales staff Energy and fun in the office Regular get-togethers (every 2 months)
	To brush up coaching skills		
	To learn how to plan a large-scale project	To deliver the Chameleon project on time (organisational responsiveness)	Project team in place by May Project parameters signed off by Board in July
Private goals	To learn how to identify and present information that Mike (boss) requires	To establish a solid working relationship with Mike	More trust, he keeps me informed Regular meetings (fortnightly) Agreement about how he involves himself in Chameleon
	To be better able to structure presentations	To build own self-confidence	To feel able to speak up at Board level To enjoy public speaking

Diagram 11. Programme goals matrix.

outcomes from the coaching are in their best interest. However, the player may wish to keep some goals private and confidential with the coach. I am thinking here of issues such as self-confidence and difficult working relationships, for example with the player's line-manager. To satisfy both these needs the matrix is divided in two by a horizontal line. Above the line are the public goals. These can be communicated to the player's line-manager and a representative from the Human Resource department for their input and agreement. This is a process that I strongly recommend as it increases the effectiveness of the coaching through having better quality goals and can ensure that the player is given feedback that might otherwise be missed. Below the line are the private goals. As a matter of integrity these private goals must contribute to the player's performance within the organisation, as the coaching is being paid for by the organisation and takes place in working hours.

Generating success criteria

Let me tell you the story of Kevin. I was coach and manager at a small tennis centre in Ireland that was situated beside a large housing estate. The estate had been built on the outskirts of the city to house a former inner city community. Their original houses had been torn down to make room for office blocks and shops. As with many such developments, the uprooted community developed more than their fair share of problems. There was a high unemployment rate and the attendant violence and drink and drug problems.

On one particular Friday, shortly after the schools had broken up for the summer holidays a boy about twelve years old appeared at the tennis centre. He watched everything that was going on and gravitated towards the court where I was working. I was coaching a client in the serve. All the balls had been hit down to the other end of the court so I turned to collect them and almost tripped over the boy. He had collected all the balls into the basket and brought them back to me. Without a word he then ran back to the other end of the court. Some minutes later all the balls had been used up but the client needed to quickly hit some more. I looked to the boy who was at the other end of the court. He took a ball and threw it the length of the court straight into my hand. I said nothing, put the ball in my pocket and held out my hand. Thwack. Another ball, straight into the palm of my hand. I looked at the client. This frail-looking boy, with a great big grin, had an elegance of technique and a rhythm that you seldom see. His name was Kevin. He had played tennis once before with an aunt. He had enjoyed it and would like to try again. He spent the rest of the day helping me during the lessons.

The next day we had a tennis lesson. He learned very quickly. It was a Saturday and there were a lot of people about. Pretty soon there was small crowd around the court. It was not just that he had talent and a grace about his movement, he had a joy about him that was infectious. At the end of the summer Kevin had made remarkable progress. He had also seen some of the better tennis players in his age group working out at the centre. Next year he wanted to play a few tournaments. I agreed to coach him over the winter and in exchange he was to keep part of the centre tidy. In making our agreement I asked him what his goals were. He wanted to qualify for the national championships and win his first round match in the next year. That would have put him in the best 32 players in his age group – a stretch goal if I had ever seen one.

Kevin worked hard over the next year, often coming to the centre before school to get in some extra practice. The tennis centre had never been so tidy. Unbelievably he qualified for the nationals. I had a business meeting when his first-round match was on and did not get to see it. I got to the club just as the result was posted. He had won. It took me some time to find him. He was in an annexe to the changing room and had been crying.

'What's wrong? You won, didn't you?'

'Yes', his voice shaking.

'So what?s wrong?'

'It was a bad match. I felt tense the whole time. We were both angry; I could see it in his face. And I used a bad word. And he called me a bad name. I don't want to play like that.'

'So how do you want to play?'

He relaxed a little. 'I want to feel relaxed and calm, like when we play.'

'What else?'

'And I want to feel the ball in the centre of my racket. I want us both to be happy, smiling. And I want be able to say "good shot" when he hits a good shot.'

'Is that how you want to play your next match?'

'Yes.'

Kevin lost his next match. But it was a great victory for him. He played beautifully and gave full expression to who he was.

Kevin's original goal was very clear by most criteria. It was specific, measurable, realistic (if a bit of a stretch) and had a clear end date - to reach the second round of the nationals next year. But we had missed something critical and had stumbled onto an interesting additional technique in resolving it. When Kevin told me what had gone wrong and then translated it into how he wanted it to be, everything was described in terms of things that he could either see, hear or feel. When you think about it, if you cannot detect something through your senses then it does not exist. It is a figment of your imagination. If you take the time to translate goals or objectives into what you can see, hear and feel – and I guess smell if you must – then you will identify two additional aspects of the goal. This technique is invaluable when filling in the third column of the programme goals matrix.

In a coaching session using this technique might sound like:

COACH So what is your longer-term goal for your time management?

PLAYER   If I could get to a position, within the next month, where I am saving three hours a week, am processing less paper and get the weekly reports out on time, that would be just great.

COACH   And when you have successfully achieved that how will you know? What would you see that would be different?

PLAYER   Three times a week I'd get home earlier.

COACH   And what would you see? What would be the evidence?

PLAYER   The evidence would be me, my body, standing in the kitchen with the clock saying six o'clock and not seven.

COACH   And what would you hear?

PLAYER   I'd hear the kids laughing and playing, because they would still be up. And, on a good day, my wife saying, 'you're home early, that's nice'. And she'd be happy to see me.

COACH   What would you see, actually if she was happy?

PLAYER   A smile.

COACH   And what would you feel?

PLAYER   More relaxed.

COACH   How else would you know?

Making a goal or objective as 'real' as the example above gives some clear measures, confirmation that it is the right goal and typically deepens the desire to achieve it. I suppose it is appropriate that the chapter on getting started should finish with observations about goals and success measures, for the only real measure of the effectivess of coaching lies in the achievement of goals.

'Getting started' in coaching, the initial sessions where the goals are agreed, the contract formed, a relationship of trust begun and the organisation's needs accounted for, can occur as a somewhat tedious part of the process. Overlook it at your peril, for it is the foundation of a successful relationship.

Chapter 10
Coaching teams

So far in this book the attention has been on the coaching of individuals. It does not take much imagination to begin to wonder how this approach and these skills might affect teams. Many organisations have invested time and money in developing teamwork in the hope that it will increase performance. No doubt there will have been some benefit to the bottom-line in some cases, but the vast majority of team building and team development exercises flounder – as the raft they have built hits the rapids. The 'outward bound' approach almost never translates into the workplace, and 'high performance teams' become so dependent on 'process' – doing it the right way – that it leaves the individual's needs and the task itself behind. And you can stop waving your hands – of course there are exceptions. But in the main the learning, such as it is, is not sustainable. Coaching teams has a very specific intent: to ensure that the team achieves its goals. Any activity or exercise that the team undertakes must contribute to this and thus the organisation's goals. Some years ago I worked with a team that had been established to launch a new financial service. It involved the building of an entire organisation, from the people, to the systems, to the office buildings. This is team coaching at its most exciting, where it involves the delivery of tangible goals.

If coaching individuals has its difficulties and complexities then these are multiplied when coaching teams. There is a new spin to all that has been discussed so far in relation to coaching individuals that contributes to this complexity. I am talking about the obvious distinction between individual and team coaching: there are more people involved. At the surface level this means that more time is spent in the process of coaching. An individual can get to a level of clarity and make a decision relatively quickly. In a team that process takes much more time as each person needs to be heard, disagreement handled, consensus and commitment built. Now look beyond the surface, look to the interrelationships in the team, the dynamics and evolution of the team, and a whole new ball game emerges.

These issues should not scare you off coaching teams because, as will become evident, there is an inherent resource unique to teams which can produce a form of 'self-coaching' – this resource is the very human desire to be in communion. As I see it, this is a sort of Team Self Two. In this state a team can achieve extraordinary goals with minimal effort. This chapter, then, is about the inner aspect of teams. I identify some of the 'interferences' that can occur in teams and suggest a number of ways of eliminating them. The final section of the chapter is about team dynamics. This may seem like something of a detour but when understood in an inner game context I believe you will realise that these dynamics represent an unconscious drive towards Team Self Two and as such are a valuable tool in team coaching.

It is important to point out that an exclusively inner game approach is as flawed as an exclusively outer game approach. Clear goals, roles and processes (outer game) are also required. As a colleague eloquently puts it, 'You're half-assed no matter which cheek you're sitting on.'

THE INNER ASPECTS OF TEAMS

Gallwey's initial explorations into The Inner Game concerned individuals and identified the extraordinary capacity of human beings to get in their own way – self-interference. He observed that the single greatest factor that inhibits performance is human doubt (he also observed that it is somewhat odd that few, if any, psychological papers have been written on doubt). In a group situation, doubt is contagious. And as it grips it deepens, ultimately into panic. In a team, 'interference' is multiplied – no, squared – and, in the worst cases, performance diminishes to the point that one person could do the work of the team in a fraction of the time.

Some years ago I began work with a team that was in disarray. The team had a set of very challenging goals to achieve. A two-day workshop had been arranged to resolve a number of critical issues. The team had travelled to a good country house hotel in the wilds of Wales and had arrived the evening before the workshop. No excuse to be late, then. At the agreed start time, half-past eight, five of the eight team members were in the room. With mounting frustration they waited for the remaining team members. By a quarter to nine all the team members had assembled. There followed a heated argument about whether an agreed time meant the actual hour of the clock or, as three people argued, included a fifteen-minute margin. In my role as coach I could have closed down the conversation and pursued the agenda but instead I watched as the conversation went on and on. After forty-five minutes I could bear no more. Here was a group of highly intelligent individuals and a lot of interference. In this particular case the conversation about 'time' was a surrogate for a deeper issue in the team. I got to the issue, the interference, by pointing out the amount of time they had spent on a relatively unimportant issue, a symptom, and asking what they thought it was symptomatic of. At first there was no meaningful response so I imposed a minute's silence. It was a long minute. At the end of the minute one team member suggested that just perhaps within the team there were divergent opinions about a particular and important element of the vision – whether the business would pursue an Internet strategy or a telephone-based direct sales strategy. The team had fractured and aligned in two separate groups, one behind the IT Director (who was failing and losing some credibility), another behind a new arrival, an old-school retailer. We now had a pretty clear agenda for the rest of the workshop.

In the very same way that interference is either squared or multiplied so is the potential. Let me give an example. One of the places where the impact of being a great team, without interference, is immediately noticeable is in sport. When playing competitive tennis at a junior level in Ireland I joined up with another boy, Billy, who I knew only slightly, to play doubles. He was from the north side of the city of Dublin and I was from the south side. Dublin is a small city but the north–south divide is miles wide. I had not chosen to play with Billy, nor he with me. The Tennis Association decreed pairing for the sake of the inter-provincial team. We played quite well together and even won a few tournaments, but there was something missing. And then one day something different happened. I can still remember the exact moment, just as I remember the court and the people who we were playing. In the middle of a rally, without signal or spoken word, I just knew what Billy was going to do next and where he was going to move to. I noticed my body moving into open space to cover a shot without any conscious thought. The play became relaxed and spontaneous with the two of us moving, changing positions in a perfect and harmonious dance. When one made a mistake there was no sense of blame or even frustration from the other, and there was as much joy in seeing your partner hit an awesome stroke as in doing it yourself. Not only did we individually give our very best performances but we also created something unique together – a creativity in the tactics of each point that left the opponents thoroughly confused. This is an example of being a team, without interference. I know that it only involved two people, but many people report similar experiences from other activities involving greater numbers of people.

So, what was it about our team that suddenly gave us greater performance? The Inner Game model that I described earlier – Potential minus Interference equals Performance – suggests that since our team was not playing to its potential, the first thing to do is to identify the interference. Now neither Billy nor I had the understanding that would have enabled us to do that, but I will suggest a little later how we came through. Easy, of course, with hindsight. All these years later I can identify a number of aspects of interference that may well have been getting in Billy's or my way, for instance a desire to be playing with my usual partner, frustration at being forced to work with someone I had not chosen, fear of being judged, fear of letting the other down, not understanding how the other thought. And many more, I am sure. And in that rally we found relaxed concentration, a mental state in which we could perform to the best of our ability. What was different about this is that it was a shared mental state that resulted in more than either could have imagined. A kind of two squared giving four. We overcame these interferences in an entirely unconscious manner. In playing together over the summer months we had begun to trust each other and as we reached the final stages of the season our goals became more obvious and explicit. Both of these factors, as I will show later in this chapter, can be developed through team coaching.

Let me give you another example of a team that succeeded in minimising interference, to achieve flow. A colleague and I worked with a team that launched, from nothing, an innovative retail bank in the UK that became quite successful. The team leader, now the CEO of the bank, was and is a highly intelligent and intuitive man. He realised that to launch the bank on time and on budget the team would have to come together in a unique way where each individual's talents were exploited and the whole was much greater than the sum of the parts. He charged us with creating an environment in which they 'could have the difficult conversations quickly'. I remember one particular meeting where the team resolved an issue of great strategic importance in fifty minutes that the Board of the parent company had wrestled with the day before, for three hours, without coming to a solution. The team had learned to respect each other, to listen and to put aside personal agendas for the sake of the team agenda. On a really good day they did not need our coaching or facilitation; their sensitivity to each other was such that they knew instinctively who had something of value to add, and if that person was interrupted or had not been clear in what they said another member of the team would ask them to finish or ask a question to clarify the issue. It would be untrue to suggest that this team was always in flow, in Team Self Two, but they got very quick at recognising when they were not and doing whatever it took to get back into that mental state.

The purpose of creating and maintaining a team is to achieve higher performance. For a team to experience more of its potential the interference must be reduced. Interference in a team might include the following:

- Lack of trust in other team members
- Fear of ridicule
- Fear of being dominated
- Pursuit of personal agendas
- Need to lead
- Lack of clarity about the task or the goals
- Pursuit of incongruent goals
- Hidden agendas
- Not understanding (or distrusting) each other's intentions
- No agreed process for working together
- An absence of agreed ground rules
- Rivalries

- No listening
- No meaningful collective work
- Beliefs and positions (this is how things are or should be).

A team that is successful in reducing the interference will be recognisable for the following:

- An apparent absence of hierarchy in the relationships
- Listening and a desire to understand each other
- Robust, challenging conversations
- Clear feedback sought and given
- The pursuit of 'impossible' goals
- Focused activity
- An intuitive sense of where each member is and how they are doing
- Request and offers of help or support
- Flexibility in the roles and a willingness to cover for each other
- Creativity, imagination and intuition as part of the toolkit
- Team members caring for each other and their well-being
- Fun, joy and the simple pleasure of being together
- Silence and thoughtfulness before decisions and action
- Mutual accountability for the achievement of goals.

You may have noticed the correlation between the interference factors – and those characterising their absence – and the conditions of flow as described in Chapter 4.

If we consider team coaching from this perspective then the role of the team coach is, in part, to help the team to reduce the interference and to achieve a team mental state, or 'team think' as

I shall describe it. So the rest of this section of the book is devoted to that.

THE BIG THREE

There are three top-of-the-list, most-wanted elements to successful teamwork. If these are not present then the most massive interference is unleashed. To state them baldly here is almost prosaic, bordering on the self-evident, but my experience is that these three elements are almost always assumed to be obvious and clear to all concerned. The 'blindingly obvious' simply blinds and failure is imminent. These three elements are **who**, **what** and **how**.

When a group of people come together to perform a task each individual needs to understand **who** each person in the team is **what** the task is and **how** they are going to achieve it. The degree to which these things are not clear is the degree to which effectiveness is diminished.

In this context, to understand 'who each person is' means to have sufficient insight into them such that they can be trusted and their intentions are clear.

The 'what' means that there is clarity about the task facing the group: why they are doing it, and what success would look like. Interestingly, 'task' occurs at two levels. Level One is the final output, the result, the goal. Level Two is often more difficult to discern because it is concerned with what needs to be done immediately next in order to move efficiently towards the Level One goal. The team may need to address a relationship issue in the group before it can discuss what might be a more obvious issue, such as a matter of strategy. If the team fails to address the Level Two issue they will certainly come unstuck when they discuss the strategy. The interference will block their capacity to have a meaningful, creative conversation or, worse still, some people, whose buy-in may be critical, may simply 'sit on the sidelines' and at a later date claim they were never in agreement.

The 'how' is about the process of achieving the Level One aims. It concerns a wide spectrum of activities from strategy and priorities to communication, meeting frequency and agendas, and ground rules.

The degree to which these elements need to be clear, understood and agreed to is dictated by the difficulty of the task. A group meeting to decide the allocation of car parking spaces does not need the same level of insight and clarity into who, what and how that a team responsible for the rapid construction of a $300m factory does.

REDUCING INTERFERENCE IN TEAMS

The ideas expressed below are intended to give a line-manager or coach a sense of how to reduce interference in teams. This is neither a comprehensive nor an exhaustive list and the exercises can be made more sophisticated. Here I just want you to get the idea.

Creating a common vision (What)

Creating a common vision or set of goals can help to reduce interference in as much as it is tangible evidence that all the players are on the same side. The creation of the vision may also flush out disagreements about the direction the team is taking. A discussion early on in the life of the team that sorts out such differences reduces internal bickering and upset. Creating a common vision can be approached in hundreds of ways. The simplest is to get each individual to write down their vision or goals and then read them out to the team. Other members of the team listen and when the readings are complete the coach asks the team to identify the common points and themes. The advantage of starting with the personal vision is that the disclosure begins to generate understanding and therefore relationships in the team.

Agreeing a modus operandi (way of working) (How)

Once the vision and goals have been agreed, the team then needs to discuss how they will achieve them. The potential for friction within the team can be greatly reduced by creating an agreement about how the individuals will cooperate. The question for the coach to ask here is 'what are the ground rules that would support this team in achieving its goals?'. Start capturing the suggestions on a flipchart without engaging in debate or assessment. When the team has run out of suggestions, get them to select those ground rules that they are all committed to. These should be reviewed at subsequent meetings and can obviously be changed, added to or removed. Ground rules might include agreements about the function and frequency of team meetings, the values that they will adhere to (honesty, respect, etc.), and when the team will decide by unanimity, consensus or team leader's decision.

Disclosure of life and career goals (Who)

This is a very simple team exercise to do and can even be done over a meal or a drink. Give the individuals some time to prepare and think through their goals – to do it properly the coach can work with the individuals prior to the meeting. The individuals then talk to the team about their personal goals. This exercise works because it builds understanding and therefore trust.

Facilitating feedback (Who, but can drag up issues of What and How)

I have already said some things about feedback in Chapter 5. Again this exercise should build understanding and trust in the group.

The simplest method is for each team member to take a turn in the 'hot chair'. The other members of the team then give the individual feedback. A standard format to the feedback can make this easier. For example:

One thing I would like you to stop doing is …
One thing I would like you to start doing is …
One thing I would like you to continue doing is … .

Identification of internal and external obstacles (Who, What and How)

This exercise is a way of getting the team to identify the interference for itself. There is more ownership this way. The question to ask the team is 'What are the obstacles, within the team or outside the team, to your success/achieving your vision?'. The coach will note down all the obstacles on a flipchart and get the team to rank-order them in terms of the impact on the team. The GROW model can then be used by the coach to resolve the issues, thus reducing interference.

Surfacing conflict

There will almost always be a tendency to avoid conflict in life and in teams. If this happens the team is stuck and no meaningful work can be done. The coach's role is to notice the conflict when it rears its head and to ensure that the team talk it through. Arranging for the parties in conflict to state clearly their position is the first step. Ensuring that the opposing party listens is the second. An option here is to get each party to state the opposing party's position. As a coach you also need to watch that the relationships survive intact, or better still deepen, as a result of the conflict. Questioning each party about how they feel about each other is a good starting point.

When a team is in conflict and is not making progress, try

declaring one minute's silence. This is a very challenging and powerful technique. The reflection that the individuals engage in during
this minute is undistracted and seems to bring them face-to-face
with their integrity. At the end of the silence someone will usually
take the risk and say what needs to be said, thus unblocking the team.

ACHIEVING 'TEAM THINK'

The story of my tennis partnership with Billy is a good example of
'team think'; we got to a point where we knew what the other was
going to do. A specific request from my client in financial services
that I mentioned earlier – to have the difficult conversations quickly
– was in effect a request to help him and his colleagues get to a similar point. His analogy was with a Rugby Football team in which
each player simply knew where their teammates were and so could
pass the ball without even looking. In fact there came a time in this
team when I as the coach was almost redundant because the team
members were so aware of each other and took such care of each
other that they were coaching themselves. This state of team think
is achievable and requires some effort. But even making progress on
the road to team think pays immediate and noticeable dividends.
This next section should give you further insight into this notion.

The stages of development of teams

There is some really good news about coaching teams, and specifically about reducing interference. It is this: most people want to be
in relationships with those around them. And they want the relationships to be meaningful. Now, they may have to unlearn some
stuff before they can have those relationships but at least as a coach
you should know that, in this sense at least, you are working with
gravity and not against it. There is something instinctive at work

that guides people towards greater union. I do not particularly want to get spiritual about it but I guess it is a higher expression of what we are as human beings. As a team develops and the individuals gain greater understanding of each other the team passes through four stages. There are two relatively well-known models that describe this process. The one best known in the workplace is:

Forming ➤ Storming ➤ Norming ➤ Performing

A less well-known model is

Pseudocommunity ➤ Chaos ➤ Emptiness ➤ Community

Both these models have a lot to offer and are quite similar. The second model is from a book by M. Scott Peck called *The Different Drum*. His book is about communities, not teams, but the process the team goes through is similar.

Stage One. When a team comes together for the first time, even if some of the members know each other, there is an unconscious game in play. The outcome from the game is that everyone should get on and that there should be no disagreement. The members play the game by a set of rules that preserve this balance. In order to preserve the balance, people pretend. They pretend that they agree with each other, they tell half-truths and little lies. It is like being at a party with people whom you do not know. 'Isn't the garden lovely?', a guest says. It is awful, and you both know it, and you hear your voice say, 'Yes, they must work so hard on it'. This is not the atmosphere of a high-performing team, but it is where all teams start. In the workplace the ground rules are different but the game is the same. Everyone knows that George is manipulating the meeting but the only time it gets mentioned is in the pub. Very little that gets said in the pub ever changed anything – and not just because it is not often remembered! In order for a team to be productive it must move out of this pretence and get to a place where the truth can be told and where people can be all of who they are. But there are one or two steps on the way.

Stage Two. Individual differences are not permitted in Stage One but as the team sets about its task differences will arise. As these surface the team moves into a phase where disagreement, conflict and confusion prevail. The tendency at this point is often to retreat into Stage One, pretence. Another thing that happens at this point is that the team members fight it out, trying to ensure that one version of the truth dominates, and try to convert each other to their own point of view. From this place, again no useful work can be done. The coach's job is to ensure that the team does not do that, but rather faces up to the differences. As the coach you need to be attentive to a typical response of teams in chaos: they will blame you for it – 'You should have been a stronger facilitator.'

Stage Three. This stage is the most difficult for the team to tolerate. In order for the team to progress, the individual members have to be willing to give up on their version of the truth, or reality, or the right solution. They have to be willing to embrace another person's point of view, or even their right to have a point of view. The second model is a more useful guide here. Teams will try to escape from chaos by imposing an order on things: they will establish project teams or sub-committees to come back with a recommendation. That is all very well as far as it goes but the team is still left with unresolved differences that are now probably even more difficult to get on the agenda. The first model does not serve us well here in that the danger of 'Norming' is that it is simply another version of Stage One: pretence. To move on, the coach works with the team so that they listen to each other, acknowledge their differences and learn to look at issues from the perspective of another. A powerful technique to use when there is a conflict is to get one party to sum-marise the other's position and then the second party does the same thing. It flushes out misunderstandings but more importantly forces each party to understand the other's point of view. Once a team has completed this 'Emptiness' stage, it is as if all the interfer-ence evaporates and the team can enter Stage Four.

Stage Four. The experience of this final phase can be very profound for the team. The team is there, fully present, not knowing and without a personal agenda or any attempt to win someone over. From here something magical can happen and the team can focus on its task. It is a space of creativity, insight and imagination where it is possible to see an issue as it really is. Decisions can be made clearly and easily; a new vision can be created with the full align-ment of the whole team. The atmosphere in the room will be quiet, with a bubbling of joy and excitement just below the surface. One of the signs that the team is in this stage is the reluctance of the team members to leave the room when the meeting is over. This is part-ing-is-such-sweet-sorrow and should be indulged.

Once the team has achieved Stage Four it will carry that spirit with it for quite some time and it will infect others that the mem-bers touch. However, the team will not stay in this space. Stage Four will, after a while, become Stage One again and the whole process recommences. Far from being bad news, this is the opposite. Each time the team passes through the stages the relationships deepen and become more resilient and trusting. The team, with help from the coach, also learns how to go through the stages, gets quicker at it and becomes more skilled in reaching 'team'.

There are at least two ways in which a coach can use this informa-tion. The first is to simply notice the progress through the stages and let the model guide your interventions, and not to panic when it gets sticky. Stage Two is uncomfortable but essential. The second way is to reveal the model to the team and to talk it through with them. This will give them some security in the chaos stage and give them useful information in how to move forward. Sometimes, when I have spoken about the model and the team that I am working with gets stuck, someone will ask, 'Is this chaos?' The very knowledge that it is allows them to persevere.

THE GROW MODEL IN TEAM COACHING

Imagine that you have just walked into a team coaching session. You are there as an observer. The team meeting has already started and has had a brief conversation around the topic but you haven't missed anything. This team is composed of the managers of the IT department in a retail bank. So IT is really important. Let me tell you who's in the room; from the left we have Sally, then Tom, Peter, Jucintha and Frank. Frank is running the project. The coach is also the line-manager, although some report through Frank.

COACH   Let me just check my understanding. As a result of our last meeting you went out and collected feedback from your internal customers. There are many good points in the feedback, like the quality of your solutions. The main area for improvement is in the quality of the service you provide. Is that correct so far?

PETER   Yes. Pretty much.

COACH   Tell me what the specific feedback is.

TOM   The two main areas are that while the quality of most of what we deliver is seen as excellent, we are almost always late in delivery. In one particular case by six months.

SALLY   Hold on. It's not that simple. The customer kept changing their mind.

PETER   Then you should have changed the delivery date …

COACH   It sounds like there might be something to discuss there but let's not get into the detail yet. Tom, you said there were two areas …

TOM   Yes. The other area is that some of what we have delivered has not matched the customer's need. Now in one case at least they did not discover this until the software was installed. And this is not a quality issue, the software works, it just doesn't meet all the requirements.

COACH   Were there any other significant points raised in the feedback?

SALLY   I think that one thing people are asking for is more support in the handover of systems and, if possible, for a short time afterwards.

PETER   You know we can't give that. We're short-staffed as it is.

SALLY   Well, it's what the customer wants.

COACH   Given all of that, what would be a useful goal for this session?

FRANK   I want to know what we are going to do about it.

COACH   Fine. So what would be a goal for the session?

JUCINTHA   Maybe we could create an action plan to improve customer services.

TOM   We'd have to have an idea about what improved customer services would look like. A vision or some goals.

PETER   That's all very well. But it seems to me that we've got a problem already. I'd like to understand that first.

COACH   I have heard three goals: to create an action plan, to have a vision or some goals and to understand the current problem. Is that right?

FRANK   We could do all of that, I think. At least it's worth a try.

SALLY   OK.

COACH   Is everyone on board for the three goals?

VOICES   Yes.

COACH   Peter, what about you?

PETER   I think it's a lot to tackle. We always take on too much.

COACH   Are you willing to give it a go?

PETER   OK, but I'd like to start with examining the current problem.

COACH   Thank you. We've got our goals. And Peter would like to start with the current problem. Is that the best place to start?

JUCINTHA   It's as good as any.

COACH   So what is the current problem?

PETER   The way I see it certain people over-promise to the client. And that means that we end up not delivering what was expected or being late. We have to manage the customer's expectations.

COACH   When you say certain people, who specifically do you mean?

PETER   Sally mostly. And sometimes Frank. But other than me they are the only two people who agree work. So that has a big impact on the team.

SALLY   We keep having this conversation. I say that you do everything you can to give the customer what he wants and exceed his expectations.

COACH   That sounds like a pretty fundamental disagreement. Before we get into it, are there any other aspects of this issue?

JUCINTHA   I think we are understaffed. We need at least one more person. A programmer.

FRANK   I believe that the budgeting process is getting in our way. We hold some of the budget, the development bit, and the customer holds the implementation part. It makes negotiation very difficult.

COACH   So we've got a disagreement about what we offer the customer, a question about staffing and a budgeting issue. Which of these should we tackle first?

SALLY   I am tired of the battle with Peter. I'd like to get that out of the way.

COACH   Battle. That's a strong word.

SALLY   Well it's what it feels like. Every time we start up a project Peter attacks me.

COACH   Have you told him that?

SALLY   I think so.

COACH   To be sure, why don't you tell him now?

SALLY   Peter, you are constantly attacking me over what you call over-promising and I call delivering a great service.

COACH   What is the effect of that on you?

SALLY   It's exhausting and very frustrating. And if I am truthful I can get quite upset.

PETER   I didn't realise. I'm sorry.

SALLY   OK.

COACH   I don't know if you guys need to do anything to restore good will or whatever.

SALLY   Maybe. Off-line. Later.

PETER   Yes. We can fix a time.

COACH   OK. And we are still left with the issue; what we offer the customer. I understand the over-promising part. What's the alternative?

PETER   You've got to manage the customer's expectations down. The budget is limited, there's only a certain amount of time and very often the technology isn't available.

TOM   I understand that but my heart is with Sally. The job would become really boring if we just delivered the minimum. I need the challenge. I enjoy problem solving and the opportunity to be creative.

SALLY   That's exactly what I think.

PETER   But if you do that we all end up exhausted and constantly overstretched. And then you create more work by having to return to the customer to fix some part that didn't get dealt with properly the first time. More work.

TOM   Do you understand that that seems boring to many of us?

PETER   No. Well, of course. But don't think that I'm just some kind of boring bean counter. I get satisfaction from delivering something that works.

COACH   Frank, where are you in this?

FRANK   I can see both points of view. I've just been thinking that what's going to matter in six months time is what our customers think of us. Because when the new performance management system comes on line that is how our performance will be judged.

JUCNTHA   Can I say something? I don't think it matters whether Peter or Sally is right. I think that the customer is more important. I'm sorry to say this but I sometimes think that Sally is so interested by the technology that she forgets the customer and that Peter is so concerned about well, how shall I say it, getting the balance between home and work right, that he'll deliver the least he can get away with.

PETER   Another way of saying that is that Sally and I are concentrating on fulfilling our own needs and not the customer's. Right?

JUCINTHA   Maybe. I don't want to upset anyone.

TOM   It's an interesting point. What would have to change?

SALLY   We'd all have to focus more on the customer.

COACH   And what would that look like?

FRANK   Giving them what they want, what they really need.

COACH   How would you go about doing that?

SALLY   Spend more time talking with them.

PETER   Better analysis of the problem or need.

TOM   Being prepared to say 'no'.

COACH   Any other options?

JUCINTHA   Involving them more in the development of the software.

PETER   I wonder, maybe on bigger projects, if we could get people seconded to our own team?

SALLY   The advantage in that, for the customer, is that one of their own team becomes the expert and they would be less reliant on us. And we would be certain to get a better understanding from the customer's perspective.

COACH   Any more thoughts? No? So which of these options do you want to take forward?

FRANK   All of them, I think. But can we just hold off making a plan at this point. I'd still like to do the vision and that may alter the plan.

TOM   Good idea.

COACH   Ready to move on?

THE MODEL T IN TEAMS

The concept of 'following interest' in teams may be difficult to grasp, what with so many different and potentially divergent agendas. The Model T as described in Chapters 3 and 4 proves to be a magnificently powerful technique in this situation. The model says that you expand before you focus and in this manner you stay on the player's agenda. I will take a snippet from the conversation above to demonstrate this:

COACH   It sounds like there might be something to discuss there but let's not get into the detail yet. Tom, you said there were two areas … [Expanding/clarifying]

TOM   Yes. The other area is that some of what we have delivered has not matched the customer's need. Now in one case at least they did not discover this until the software was installed. And this is not a quality issue; the software works, it just doesn't meet all the requirements.

COACH   Were there any other significant points raised in the feedback? [expanding again]

And then a little later:

COACH   I have heard three goals; to create an action plan, to have a vision or some goals and to understand the current problem. Is that right?

FRANK   We could do all of that, I think. At least it's worth a try.

SALLY   OK.

COACH   Is everyone on board for the three goals?

VOICES   Yes.

COACH   Peter, what about you?

PETER   I think it's a lot to tackle. We always take on too much.

COACH   Are you willing to give it a go?

PETER   OK, but I'd like to start with examining the current problem.

COACH   Thank you. We've got our goals. And Peter would like to start with the current problem. Is that the best place to start? [focusing]

JUCINTHA   It's as good as any.

COACH   So what is the current problem?

Coaching teams, indeed the whole issue of teamwork is so huge that this chapter can only serve as an introduction. I hope, however, that it has been more than an introduction and that you feel that you could make a start – and a difference – by coaching either the team that you lead or one that you are coach to, such as a project team that you are looking after. The key is to get started. You can only learn to coach by coaching.

Chapter 11
Coaching in context

The last chapter was different from the greater part of the book in that it shifted the focus from the individual to the team. This chapter makes a similar shift and brings the organisation into focus and in so doing picks up on one of the ideas of Chapter Eight, the relationship between the individual and the organisation. Because no individual exists in isolation. Each person, each player, operates in a context, and for most people in business, that context is the organisation. In Chapter 8 I put forward the notion that to be effective as either a line-manager or a coach it is not sufficient to simply help the individual player become more effective – you must also ensure that the increase in effectiveness contributes towards the achievement of the organisation's goals. Clearly a large part of this is achieved through the coaching itself ('Tell me, how will this course of action contribute to the organisation achieving its goals?'). But I am also suggesting that the capacity of the line-manager or the coach to understand the organisational context in which the player is operating adds much to the coaching. This capacity might also be called consulting, the mention of which suddenly introduces a new, major topic. However, it is not my intent here to present a complete guide to consulting. What I do want to do is to give you two things, a holistic approach to understanding organisations and an introduction to a critical skill: that of generating and testing hypotheses.

In Diagram 5 (Chapter 5) I identify one of the skill sets required for effective coaching as being 'Understanding organisational context' and I suggest that the intent is *to ensure that the coaching engage-*

ment meets the client's needs. One of the distinctions that I have been at pains to make is between the player and the client. To remind you, the client is the organisation itself and typically there will be someone representing the organisation – the person who pays the bill. The client's (or the organisation's) needs will almost always be either different from, or greater than, the individual's, and in order for the coaching to be successful these different needs have to be accounted for within the coaching intervention.

THE FOUR QUADRANTS

There are two big themes in this book that I want to bring together here in order to provide a lens through which you might view an organisation. The first of these themes is the idea of Inner and Outer, and the second is the notion of the Individual and the Organisation. Bringing them together is most easily done diagrammatically (see Diagram 12). I draw a vertical line to show the Inner/Outer divide and a horizontal one to show the Individual/Organisational divide, thus producing four quadrants. This then suggests that not only does an individual have an Inner and an Outer (an example of Inner is a belief; an example of Outer is skill), as already put forward, but that an organisation also has an Inner and an Outer, e.g. values (Inner) and performance management systems (Outer). I explain this diagram more fully later in this chapter.

In order to understand these four quadrants more completely I have to take you back to the source (much as I would like to claim it as my original thinking). The four quadrants are presented in a book called *A Brief History of Everything* by Ken Wilber. He makes different but congruent distinctions to define the quadrants (Diagram 14). In the place of Inner and Outer he uses Interior and Exterior, and in the place of Organisational he uses Collective.

INNER | OUTER

Sense of purpose/meaning Aspirations Desires Attitudes Beliefs Personal values	Goals Plans Skills Behaviours

INDIVIDUAL
ORGANISATIONAL

Mission	Vision Organisational goals Strategy
Culture Organisational values	Behavioural norms Code of conduct
	Performance management systems Management information systems
Corporate mindset	

Diagram 12. The four quadrants (adapted from Ken Wilber, *A Brief History of Everything*).

Left-hand side	Right-hand side
Interior Subjective Depth Intentional Mind	*Exterior* Objective Surface Behavioural Brain

Diagram 13. Left-and right-hand sides.

INTERIOR | EXTERIOR

Freud (internal life) Truthfulness	Skinner (behaviour) Truth

INDIVIDUAL
COLLECTIVE

Kuhn (interpretation) Justness	Marx (collective social systems) Functional fit (justice system)

Diagram 14. The four quadrants (adapted from Ken Wilber, *A Brief History of Everything*).

These are perhaps some of the simplest distinctions a human being can make; inside and outside, singular and plural. Let me try to bring this to life through a number of different routes. I will start by making some distinctions between Interior (left-hand side) and Exterior (right-hand side) – see Diagram 13.

- Subjective and Objective. The content of our experience that is subjective belongs on the left-hand side, the objective on the right.
- Depth and Surface. Surface is on the right-hand side. Surface can be seen. Something exists, you can see it or feel it. Depth is on the left-hand side. It can only be revealed in conversation and must be interpreted to be understood.
- Intentional and Behavioural. Intention is about meaning and purpose (left-hand side) and behaviour is what flows from that (right-hand side).
- Mind and Brain. A brain surgeon deals with the physical form of the brain (right-hand side), a psychologist with the mind (left-hand side).

Diagram 14 in which I put back the horizontal line and the Individual/Collective split shows the following points:

- Freud was concerned with the internal life of individuals (upper left), B.F. Skinner with the behaviour of individuals (upper right), Thomas Kuhn with how a shared, background context governs interpretation (lower left) and Karl Marx with collective social systems (lower right).
- Truth (upper right) is verifiable, i.e. empirical truth as in 'it's raining outside'. Truthfulness (upper left) is about trust – when I tell you it's raining outside do you believe me? Justness (lower left), in the collective sense, is a commonly held context about whether something is right or not. Functional fit (lower right), represents the justice system, i.e. the framework of law and its process.

What this last bullet-point is intended to reveal is the idea that what occurs in one quadrant is reflected in them all. For instance a community's, or a nation's, sense of justness needs to be reflected in the justice system; a disconnection here can cause much unhappiness and even outrage.

Wilber illustrates this connectedness with an example, which I present here in my own words. Imagine an anthropologist visiting a North American Hopi Indian tribe and observing a rain dance. He would describe this objectively as a set of behaviours that have some function in the social system (lower right). A social psychologist visiting the tribe might enquire into the meaning of the dance and why it is valued in the community (lower left). Both investigators will arrive at different understandings *both of which are valid* and, when taken together, add to the richness of the overall understanding. As an aside, all too often we exclude one or other side from our understanding. B.F. Skinner held that one could never understand what was going on inside an individual, that the mind was a 'little black box' and that we therefore should not bother trying, leaving us with a literally one-sided behavioural psychology that has translated into a limited, 'carrot-and-stick' approach to motivation in many organisations.

Let me stretch the analogy a bit further. Say one of our investigators picked on an individual participant in the dance and asked what the meaning of the dance was for that person (upper left). Assuming that the individual was a healthy, engaged member of the community, the response might be: 'See the man leading the dance: he's my father and our Chief. He's retiring at the end of the year and I have to step into his shoes.' So for this individual there is a meaning to the dance that is unique but also congruent with the collective meaning. What's more, the individual meaning will almost certainly translate into a different set of behaviours for that individual – he'll have to learn how to lead the dance (upper right). What occurs in one quadrant is reflected in them all.

The intent in the last few paragraphs has been to give you some sense of the richness of Wilber's work before I transpose the model into the organisational context (Diagram 12).

THE FOUR QUADRANTS IN ORGANISATIONS

- The upper left quadrant concerns the inner life of the individual: his or her sense of purpose, their aspirations and desires, their attitudes and beliefs and their personal values.
- The upper right quadrant is about the way in which the upper left manifests in the world: the individual's goals and the plans and strategies that flow from the goals. It also concerns their skills and behaviours, and even their mannerisms.
- The lower left quadrant concerns the inner life of the organisation: its mission, culture, values, the corporate mindset - what people believe is possible and not possible.
- The lower right quadrant is about the external representation of the lower left: the organisation's vision, goals and strategies - the collective behavioural norms, the code of conduct. It also embraces the systems that facilitate the management of the organisation.

In the same way as we extended our perspective from the individual to the team and now to the organisation, it is to be remembered that the organisation too sits within a context that is social and economic, meaning that the model can be expanded to embrace these things. I will limit our scope here to the organisation itself in the hope of making the principles clear.

I said a little earlier that anything that occurs in one quadrant is reflected in all four and illustrated this with the Hopi Indians example. This idea provides two keys for using this model as a diagnostic tool to understand what might be going on in an organisation. The first key is about presence: if I observe some aspect of the organisation then I must ask myself in what way is it present in the other quadrants. The second key is congruence: for instance, an individual may have a desire (Diagram 11, top left, inner individual), something they want to achieve. The individual will need to take actions or have a plan (top right, outer individual) to achieve that desire. The actions or plan could lead him towards that desire or away from it. The actions that lead towards the desire are deemed congruent with the desire. So having observed something in one quadrant you need to see how it occurs in the other quadrants and then check that there is congruence. Be clear that this is no academic exercise – if it is not present, or is present and not congruent, failure ensues.

Imagine coaching an individual who has a need for acknowledgement (top left) and this is expressed as a desire for promotion in the organisation. Imagine too that they are acting and behaving (top right) in such a way that they are upsetting the people they manage and not achieving the performance goals they have achieved with their line-manager. Looking at this through the lens of the four quadrants you might notice the following:

- The actions and behaviours (top right) are not congruent with the expressed desire (top left).
- The actions and behaviours are not congruent with the organisational culture (bottom left).
- The individual goals (top right) are not congruent with the goals of the organisation (bottom right).

Failure is imminent. As a coach, standing back and noticing these things is a vital activity. You might then choose to bring your observation to the attention of the coach. I suggest how you might do that in the section below on hypothesising

Let me develop these ideas of Presence and Congruence with two illustrations. The first is a series of observations about the reasons behind why it is so difficult to change the culture of an organisation; the second is an (illuminating, I hope) anecdote about just such an initiative that was successful.

Most organisations now have some sort of statement about their corporate values. And in most cases they make absolutely no difference to what happens on a day-to-day basis. The four quadrants can help in understanding why the values do not 'live'. Corporate or organisational values occur in the lower left quadrant. They are most often generated, or at least endorsed, by the leadership group in the organisation. It is fairly easy to check out whether these individuals 'walk the talk' (i.e. the values are *present* in the upper right): whether the leadership group behaves in a manner *congruent* with the expressed values. If they do not then the values are doomed from the start. Now check out whether the values are reflected in the performance management system (lower right). More and more you will find that they are, but move on to the remuneration system and, again in most cases, you will find that people are not specifically rewarded for upholding the values and thus the values do not enter into the day-to-day running of the business. Teamworking is a value that you will frequently see in value statements but is not reflected in the pay packet.

However, I suggest that the biggest reason why values fail to take root in most organisations is the schism between the lower left and the upper left; between what an individual's personal values are and the expressed values of the organisation. This occurs in two ways. The leadership group that generated the values was not creating them for themselves *but for everyone else*; so of course they then don't 'walk the talk' ('Teamwork is a good thing but I'll run my department as I see fit'). Secondly, for the majority of the staff the values are imposed on them and bear little or no relation to what the individual's values actually are; a failure to align the personal with the organisational prevents the values from coming to life.

Many years ago I was part of a team that undertook a project with a leading retailer in the UK to create a shift in the culture. We designed a process which had coaching at its heart and which took the programme to each store and to each individual. The first step in the process was to get the staff to identify what was important to them, what made working in that store special. Only when this was done, when each individual had had their say, was the notion of values introduced and the executive team's values presented. We then asked the store staff to compare what they thought was important and special with the executive team's value statement. The congruity surprised everyone involved, but more importantly the values now had real meaning. What was in the lower left was reflected in the upper left. Of course, there was not a one hundred percent overlap, but we had set up a communication channel to the executive that allowed for discussion about the differences, and in at least one case the executive reversed an earlier decision to charge customers for shopping bags, a decision that the staff thought inconsistent with both their own values and the values they thought the organisation should hold. This dialogue was one of the critical elements in the programme because it confirmed that all parties were taking the matter of values seriously.

My second illustration concerns a consulting project that I was lucky to be involved in. Some years ago I was given the opportunity by a consultancy to join their team working on a project with a large manufacturer of computer chips. A new factory was being built in Ireland and there was great concern for the safety of the workers. Our task was to help them create an injury-free environment. In an early phase of the project we held a workshop with the leadership group made up of representatives from the client, the management team, the contractors, the sub-contractors, service providers and so on. We asked them to list everything that was happening on the building site that was designed to increase safety. Long lists emerged: working procedures, emergency procedures, planning techniques, training, safety officer patrols, signs and barriers. When the items on the lists were plotted onto the four quadrants there was almost nothing on the left-hand side of the page! All of the activities and procedures were and are valid and vital, but this was only half the story. I remember in particular the recommendation for what should be done to stop workers from standing on the top rungs of ladders: paint them red (the ladders, that is). That's a right-hand side solution. But there was no enquiry into why workers would stand on the top rung when they knew it was dangerous. It also emerged that workers for one contractor would not intervene when they saw someone from another contractor doing something that was either obviously foolhardy or in contravention of the procedures. There was some unwritten rule that said you could not cross boundaries between employers, regardless of the potential cost, i.e. someone's life.

While the procedures and training, all the things on the right-hand side, are important, they are useless if the left-hand side issues are not addressed. Safety is predominantly about attitude and culture. When we started working on this project the prevailing attitude to safety was that 'accidents happen' (i.e. they are not caused – so they cannot be avoided and no one is responsible) and 'they don't happen to me'. I recommend that you do not go on a site visit with someone with these beliefs. Changing this mindset was the task before our team and was therefore the thrust of our activities. For the record, on completion of the project there had been the greatest number of hours worked without a significant injury in the company's history.

There is a vast richness in this model and there are many ways of using it. As I said earlier it is a lens through which to view an organisation. When working with an individual on a one-on-one basis, as either a line-manager or a professional coach, it is a relatively simple exercise to use the four quadrants to map out the details of each of the elements shown in Diagram 12 and to check for what is present and what is congruent. I have also presented the diagram to teams that I have worked with and had them complete it. However, it is most powerful when used in conjunction with the skills that I present in the next section: developing and testing hypotheses.

GENERATING AND TESTING HYPOTHESES

The example I gave earlier of the individual seeking promotion and the two further illustrations will, I hope, have shown how the four quadrants and the keys of Presence and Congruence can be a powerful diagnostic tool, a lens through which to view an organisation. Translating whatever insights or observations that emerge from using this tool into something that is valuable for the player and the organisation in which she works is the subject of this section. This skill comprises generating and then testing hypotheses.

The ideas in this section are more obviously of importance to the professional coach, whose perspective of the organisation from the viewpoint of an outsider, but with an intimate insight gained through coaching, should be a prized commodity by both organisation and coach. I would also argue that for any senior manager in an organisation, a capacity to understand what is going on is a vital skill, not just for the development of their own career but also for the organisation as they engage in conversations about strategy, new products and services, etc.

A hypothesis is a supposition or theory, a provisional explanation, developed from the available evidence or facts. The purpose in developing a hypothesis is to provide focus to any attempts to understand the organisation. Our purpose, as coaches and line-managers coaching their direct reports, in understanding the organisation is to ensure that the coaching is effective and contributes to the organisation achieving its goals. Once a hypothesis has been generated the next step is to test it for accuracy.

In my earlier example of the individual seeking promotion I might generate a number of hypotheses. It is important to note that a hypothesis does not need to be right. You also need to know that I have made up the following:

- The individual's desire is not clear to them. Is it about acknowledgement or perhaps about gaining attention (because at this they are succeeding)?

- The individual's values that give rise to overtly and aggressively seeking promotion are at odds with the organisational values where patronage is the key.

I could now test my hypotheses in a number of ways:

- I could simply outline them to the player (as long as there was sufficient trust).
- I could develop a set of questions (e.g. how do people get promoted here?) and ask various people for their observations.
- I could keep the ideas in the back of my mind and see if more collaborating evidence emerged in further conversations.

It is worth pointing out that I almost never engage in one-on-one coaching without having spoken to the player's boss, their team and other representatives of the organisation. I do this for the purpose of understanding the organisational context of the player and I do it by developing and testing hypotheses.

Here is a real example. I was coach for a short period to the leadership team in a small organisation of international repute that was involved in the art world. This meant working with the three key directors on a one-on-one basis and also with them as a team. To start with I spent some time in the organisation meeting with various members of staff in an initial induction phase. As the coaching started I found it very difficult to identify meaningful coaching goals with any of the three individuals. The first team-coaching session was very difficult as nobody was willing to acknowledge in public that there were any problems. I was left with a real problem about how the coaching intervention could add value to the organisation. As I thought about it between meetings what I most noticed was the inability of any of the people I had spoken with in the organisation to tell the truth to me, to each other or to themselves.

My initial hypothesis, therefore, was that for reasons that I had not yet grasped, straight talking and openness were absent from the organisation and thus there was no effective performance management because feedback, and the notion of holding people to account (both of which require straight talking and openness), were completely absent. In order to test this I fixed meetings with two people in the organisation with whom I felt there was sufficient trust to have a more open conversation. What emerged from these conversations was a singular fact: that the movement of many of the artifacts across international borders was, well, not entirely legal. In this environment not only did people not want to communicate what they were doing but also nobody, particularly the senior management, wanted to know. The secrecy required to keep this part of the business running infected the culture and it became impossible to be open. I would like to say that I confronted the team I was coaching and they 'fessed up and sorted it', but the stakes were too high. I did give them an opportunity to grapple with the issues by presenting a report of my findings, mentioning the culture of secrecy (but not my hypothesis about its origins – I had no proof). The opportunity was well understood but not acted upon, and I was shown the door with great gracefulness. You win some and you lose some.

Not all situations are so dramatic but in this case it would have been easy enough for me to continue with the coaching programme and to have added no discernible value, thus damaging my own reputation and sullying the good name of coaching.

Having established what I see as the benefits of generating and testing hypotheses, the key question, of course, is 'How do I go about it?' Well, in practical terms there are three stages in the generation and testing of a hypothesis (Diagram 15). These are noticing, formulating and testing.

- Noticing, as I observed earlier, is the 'not trying' of thinking. In the inner game model, trying is a major interference. Trying to

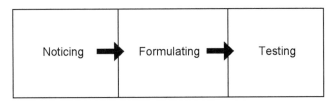

Diagram 15. Generating and testing a hypothesis.

think hurts (you have to screw up your eyes) and seldom gets you anywhere. The best ideas come when you are relaxed, often doing something entirely different. So simply take a step back and notice. Bring your attention to whatever thoughts you do have about the matter, the observations you have, your feelings, both emotional and sensory, to what your intuition is telling you and to what you imagine or fantasise.

• Formulate the shortest possible statement that brings together all that you have noticed.

• Identify all the possible sources of information that will help you test the hypothesis (people inside and outside the organisation, documents, annual reports, industry reports, etc). Testing is best done by developing a set of questions (as for the example of the individual seeking promotion) from the initial hypotheses and then asking the questions of people who might have a useful perspective. Such people might include the player, their line-manager, their team, internal customers, the HR team, other colleagues or consultants working in the organisation.

A validated hypothesis can be used in a number of ways:

• If it directly concerns the player it can be fed into the coaching conversation as part of the reality phase of the GROW model.

• It can be presented to the client for them to take forward.

• It can result in a proposition about how to rectify matters. For a professional coach this could become another engagement.

This skill may appear to be contrary to the notion of coaching in which the intent is to cause the player to think. I would hope that I have not put across a message that says coaches should not think or act upon what they think. That would be both pig-headed and foolish. If I have observations about a player's or a client's situation then it would be irresponsible to withhold them. I will refer back to this in the next chapter on the art of coaching. In bringing this chapter to a close I want to state the obvious: this is not a book on consulting skills and a few thousand words are never going to cover such a rich topic. If, however, I have conveyed the idea that individuals operate in a context, in this case an organisational context, and that it is necessary to investigate and account for that context in the coaching intervention or in the line-management of your direct reports, and if I have given an idea of how you might go about that, then the job is done.

Chapter 12
The art of coaching

I am coaching someone, a woman. We are in front of about fifty people at a conference. I have never met her before today so I know nothing of her job, the company for which she works, the nature of the business or her personal background. I am nervous and a little distracted. I want to do a good job and represent the School as best I can. The subject matter of the coaching session is complex and I am struggling to understand. I can hear in her voice that there is a little emotional energy wrapped up in the issue. I wonder if I would not have been better off if I had chosen someone else to coach. I pull my chair a little closer to her and bring my attention back to what she is saying. After a few minutes I stop her and give a summary of what I have understood so far. I can see she is a little surprised that I have understood so much, in particular some of the nuances. I ask if my summary is complete. No, I have missed this bit. And she's off again. The people in the room recede into the background and then are gone. All my attention is with her and what she is saying. There is nothing else present in my mind. She relaxes a little more. I begin to notice little things: a hesitation, a slight grimace, an impatient gesture, a quickening in the pace of the talking, a change in the breathing pattern, a change of colour in the face. I notice my own response to what I am hearing and seeing, what I think and feel about what is being said. I notice a pattern in what I am hearing and seeing, faint at first, more of an intuition. Sometimes I know what she is going to say before she says it.

And then I begin to understand. Not just the issue and its significance, but an understanding of this person, who they are and how
they are playing out this part of their life.

I ask a question. It does not feel like me asking the question. I
recognise my own voice; I can feel my jaw move but the voice
seems to be located about a foot behind my left ear and six inches
to the side. In fact a part of me seems to be located in the same place
because it is almost as if I can see from there too.

The question, the culmination of all that I have learned from this
woman about the issue, is absorbed in silence. Then a smile creeps
from the corners of her mouth towards the centre and from there
to the eyes. Something has been understood, reframed; a new possibility emerges. The coaching is over. The environment begins to
intrude. There are some questions from the floor. No one has
noticed what happened save for me and, I think, my new friend.

When I am coaching, whether it is a demonstration in public or
a conversation in a client's office, I occasionally rise above my
normal proficiency to another level of skill and insight where there
is a greater fluency and not a little joy. In Inner Game terms I am
coaching from Self Two, a mental state that can be achieved in
which one performs with excellence, where all one's faculties are
available and one's sensitivity heightened. This is pure flow.

The situation described above is typical. If my description occurs
as slightly 'magical' then I do not see it as that, although we may
have different definitions of the term. As a human being that level
of performance is available to me in any and every activity. In coaching, the player is communicating with much more than the words
being spoken and each coach is capable of picking up the messages
and processing them. In fact in every conversation we have we are
picking up these signals and including them in our responses, usually in a very unconscious manner. In Self Two our observation is
more acute, we pick up more of the messages and respond in an
uninhibited and congruent manner.

This final chapter is about the inner aspects of coaching as I experience and understand it, not as a model to be applied to the player, but as a way of maximising one's own performance. In the skills chart in Chapter 5 (Diagram 5) I refer to the skill set involved in achieving this state of flow somewhat more prosaically as Managing Self and I describe the intent as:

- to minimise the impact of the line-manager's or coach's needs, preconceptions, judgements, etc., on the player, and
- to maximise one's own performance whilst coaching.

One of the core Inner Game ideas, as described earlier, is the 'equation' Potential minus Interference equals Performance. There are two major interferences that I would like to address here:

- Trying to get it right
- The coach's possible thoughts, opinions and judgements of the player.

I am reminded of a wonderful gentleman who, while learning to coach, came to a critical point in his own learning. He was trying very hard to get it right, to do it by the book, until he realised that this effort of trying was getting in the way of focusing his full attention on the player. In his next coaching session he did focus on the player more fully and his and the player's experience of coaching was transformed; it became a fluid and seamless conversation. His comment afterwards was that the models and guidelines that we had been discussing up until that time were 'for the discipline of the novice'.

My purpose here is to make sure that when coaching you are not stuck in the purely non-directive, to free you from the potential tyranny of apparent 'rules', so that it becomes possible to do what is appropriate in that minute for that particular player and thus open the door to coaching as an art, as a form of self-expression. That coaching could be self-expression might occur as a contradiction but to me the elegant deployment of all my skills is just that. It is for this reason that this chapter is called 'The art of coaching' and also why the definition of coaching given at the beginning of Chapter 3 includes the word 'art'.

TRYING TO GET IT RIGHT

I need to make sure that we do not get too precious about non-directive coaching. To do so introduces a significant interference. There is a very delicate balance to be struck here because I do not want to give licence to those who might revert to type – or more accurately habit – and to start instructing, making suggestions, giving advice or, worse still, attempting to control. The balance is between retaining what is vital in the non-directive model (ownership, responsibility, learning, high performance) and acknowledging that the person doing the coaching has intelligence, experience, intuition and imagination that, in many cases, will almost certainly be of value to the player. Imagine withholding a really good idea from the player – that would serve no-one's interests. And so I want to debunk the notion that there is a correct way to coach. Let me start this piece with another way of looking at the different approaches to coaching (Diagram 16).

• *Level One: Following interest.* This is the fundamental approach and is the foundation of effective coaching. It is to this idea that by far the greatest part of this book has been devoted.

Level Four	Knowing	↑ Directive
Level Three	Process	
Level Two	Structure	
Level One	Following interest	↓ Non-directive

Diagram 16. A hierarchy of approaches to coaching.

- *Level Two: Structure.* There are structures in our thinking or implicit in the language we use – good/bad, past/present/future or negative/positive. Very often a player will describe a situation and will reveal only one part of the structure. For instance they will describe a current situation that is undesirable in some way. The coach then asks 'How do you want it to be?'. The structure that the coach has imposed on the conversation is present/negative moving to future/positive. To a very small degree the coach has directed the conversation here, almost certainly appropriately. Another example of structure is the GROW model. Using the GROW model is a directive act, not a non-directive one.

- *Level Three: Process.* A process is a sequence of actions or events. In coaching or therapeutic terms it is a linked series of instructions that creates a movement in the player's understanding. Examples of this are guided visualisation exercises and the co-supervision exercise in Appendix 4. A process is directed by the coach.

- *Level Four: Knowing.* By this I mean what the line-manager or coach knows. This can be factual knowledge but I also include experience, wisdom, insight and intuition at this level.

Level One is the least directive approach. With each level of the hierarchy the coaching becomes more directive. What I want to be really clear about here is that coaching from any of these levels is valid as long as it passes four tests:

- It raises awareness in the player.
- It leaves responsibility and choice with the player.
- The relationship is strong enough.
- My intent is clear.

One other thing happens as we move up through the hierarchy to the more directive approaches: it becomes more and more difficult to be *effective* (as defined in Chapter 2). In fact I argue that you have to become competent at the lower levels before moving up. The irony is that in traditional approaches you do start at the top, at Level Four. However, if you do not have some competence at Level One you are unlikely to know, when coaching from say Level Four (Knowing), whether you have taken choice and responsibility away or have simply lost your audience. You are more likely to think, 'They just didn't get it. Are they stupid?' My suggestion is that you build a strong foundation of non-directive skills and then with experience and experimenting you will be able to exploit the other levels – bearing the four tests in mind.

It is also worth stating that I believe it is impossible – and perhaps not entirely desirable – for coaching to be completely non-directive. It is impossible because the slightest flicker of concern in the eye, the faintest smile of approval will show up and be read and interpreted by the player. And so to the next major interference.

THE MINDSET OF THE COACH

The second major interference is the thoughts, opinions and judgements that the person coaching might have of the player. A part of 'managing oneself' while coaching is to be able to identify one's own 'stuff' and to deal with it appropriately. 'Stuff' may take the form of notions and judgements that are not relevant to the player. And then there will be 'stuff' that is relevant. Distinguishing one from the other is clearly critical, but even more importantly this stuff will almost certainly occur as interference for the coach, distracting him from paying full attention to the player.

One route to overcoming this interference is to have a frame of reference, a mindset to bring to the coaching. I offer the following propositions as an appropriate mindset. I want you to know that what comes next is *not* the truth. It is merely a set of propositions. I find that by holding on to these propositions and operating on the basis of them I eliminate much interference and so I am a more effective coach. I will give it to you straight first and then explain it in more depth:

- People have huge potential
- People have a *unique* map of reality – not reality itself
- People have 'good' intentions …
- … and are achieving their own objectives – perfectly – at all times.

On first reading, people find this a bit difficult to swallow. Let me take it statement by statement.

People have huge potential

Most people have a belief or a point of view about human potential. At one end of the spectrum you have the 'you can't teach an old dog new tricks' brigade. They are joined by the 'I am the way I am' and the 'why should I bother' brigades. They do not have much faith in human potential. At the other end of the spectrum you have the 'I can do anything I can dream of' brigade. When these guys are standing on a cliff, flapping their arms in a frenzied imitation of a seagull, this is cause for concern. I do not know where you stand on the spectrum; I just know you stand somewhere. I suggest that neither end of the spectrum is particularly healthy. The question that we should embrace as coaches is this. Where on the spectrum should I stand as a coach, as someone committed to another's growth, development and full expression as a human being? In the story of Kevin, my assessment at the time was that the goal he had set himself was way beyond his reach. How wrong I was. To have taken the goal from him would have been to take away part of his life, a sort of well-intentioned murder. Daniel Goleman, in his book *Emotional Intelligence*, says that recent research suggests that we are only using 0.01 percent of our mental capacities as human beings.

What? I did the ball-catching demonstration described in the early part of this book at a small conference. The volunteer was a complete klutz. I noticed myself making this judgement in the first ten seconds – just in time to put it out of my mind. When the demonstration was over the volunteer had surprised himself and the entire audience. I asked the group what they had noticed in the demonstration. The response that silenced the room was 'You believed in him, even when he didn't.'

People have a *unique* map of reality – not reality itself

You have a mental map of reality. Much of that map was created in the first few years of your life and has not been updated since. You operate to a large degree on the basis of this map. If you think of a journey you take regularly you can probably visualise the route. You have a mental map of the route. A map, such as a road map, is a representation of the surface features of a territory in the same way that a menu in a restaurant is a representation of the food available. The menu is not the food. Eating the menu will upset your stomach and the waiter. Equally the map is not the territory. People, then, have a map of reality, but it is not reality. The way you think it is, is not the way it is. The way it is is the way it is and does not particularly care what you think of it – it does not change for you. The fact that we have a map of reality – and not reality – might not matter if all our maps were the same. But this is not the case. Each person's map is different – a unique map of reality, not reality itself.

There are some people out there who think that the way they think it is, is the way it is and when they say 'if I were you …' are actually a little surprised that they are not. These people do not make good coaches.

People have 'good' intentions

'Good' is not a judgement that I, the coach, am making. It is in fact an exhortation to a non-judgemental stance. That while I may initially view something as in some sense 'bad', I should withhold the judgement and seek first to understand. It suggests that most people, the very vast majority, have good intentions. They want to be happy and fulfilled and for others to be happy and fulfilled. They want good relationships with people. They want justice for all, the ending of starvation and hunger. They have good intentions in the big things in life, and the small. I think that it is possible that out there in the world there is evil and that there are some people who are evil. I think of some of the monsters of history who perpetrated the most evil deeds. But that is a matter for the psychiatrists. You may of course receive a request to coach someone with whom your values are in conflict or be asked to work for an organisation with which your values clash. And you may choose to walk away. Back to the propositions. This third proposition is linked to the fourth, which we discuss next.

People are achieving their own objectives, perfectly, at all times

This is much more difficult. The truth is, people get what they intend (the trouble is they don't always know what they intended until they get it). This morning a neighbour told me that overnight someone had put a scratch mark along the side of his car. It was done with a sharp object, like a key. It means that the entire side of the car has to be resprayed. That represents quite a lot of money and a lot of hassle. He thinks that it was one of a group of youths who live at the other end of his road. On hearing the story I was filled with righteous anger – kids these days. Hold on, people have good intentions and are achieving their own objectives, perfectly, at all times. I cannot find the person who scratched the car and even if I could I suspect the answer to 'why did you do that?' would be 'I don't know'. But maybe the youth was with his friends and scratched the car in order to gain acceptance in the group. And maybe he achieved his objective. This does not mean that there are no consequences, even unpleasant ones. And it does not mean that the action was justified within the majority of people's understanding of reality. But it does mean that in the youth's map of reality the objective to gain acceptance had some priority.

Let me give you another example. I am thinking of the person who comes into work late and leaves early. He ignores the dress code and is surly to most of his colleagues, particularly those in management positions. His work is badly done and seldom on time. The temptation is to conclude that he is a feckless layabout. That conclusion will help neither the manager nor the individual concerned. If a person has a position on a matter, that is to say makes a judgement, then immediately and inevitably they create the opposite of that position. This is the nature of opposition. If the line-manager condemns the 'feckless layabout' as such then that person is likely to take the opposite position, 'Oh, no I am not.' – a position which they will defend with intelligence and determination. A pantomime follows (Oh yes you are. Oh no I'm not). In opposition there is no real dialogue. If the manager or coach approaches this 'layabout' on the basis of his judgements then they will not have a meaningful conversation and nothing will change.

However, if the manager or coach engages on the basis that the individual has huge potential, has a unique map of reality, has 'good' intentions and is, in fact, achieving his own objectives, perfectly, in that moment, then there is the chance for something to shift. Approach someone without judgement and with empathy and something special occurs; they may let you into their map of reality and, in sharing it with you, may see it differently and may choose to alter the map. I say 'may' because there is no guarantee. But empathy is a far stronger place from which to give feedback than condemnation. For instance, the apparently feckless layabout has an interesting recent history. He was offered a job in the department at a lower grade than previously but was promised that the department's manager would be moving on in three months and that he was in line for the position. Then there was a reorganisation and the promise was forgotten. Now nobody knows what to do with him and his problem is shuffled backwards and forwards between his manager and the Human Resource department. If you had not been willing to listen you would never have found out what lay behind his behaviour and attitude – you would have always regarded him as the feckless layabout.

A line-manager in an organisation is sometimes faced with a difficult choice: whether to invest time in understanding a 'poor performer' or 'trouble-maker' (and it can be a lot of time) or whether to start disciplinary proceedings. The four propositions above do not say that people should be shielded from the consequences of their actions. People are responsible for the results they get in life. Liberalism and authoritarianism, the traditional responses, both have the tendency to remove responsibility from the individual. Effective coaching is empathetic but does not hide from reality; rather it raises awareness of it and leaves the responsibility with the player or the member of staff. Sometimes the investment will just not be worth the potential return. That will be your call – but you might at least make that call bearing in mind my four propositions.

To reiterate, then, these four propositions are not the truth. What they represent is a mindset that may serve in those situations when you are coaching.

A GARDEN GNOME?

There is one final piece that I would like to leave you with in this chapter to help you find your own 'art' in coaching, an insight into your particular inner game. Each of us brings something unique to anything we do, not least coaching, as the four propositions indicate. Gaining an understanding of that uniqueness and of how it can influence your coaching – for influence it will – can help you considerably in becoming a more effective coach and will add to the enjoyment. Whatever your uniqueness might be, your brand of humour, your particular intelligence or your type of professionalism will show up in your coaching. Best to understand what it is and also to understand how it can influence your coaching, positively and negatively. One of my colleagues, Judith, has a wonderful coaching exercise that can produce just such insights. It involves the use of imagery, as you will see. On one memorable occasion she demonstrated the exercise, with me as the player, in front of a group of senior civil servants. It went something like this.

JUDITH   Myles, if you would just relax and close your eyes. And I want you to identify an occasion when you were coaching. Have you got a situation?

MYLES   Yes, I am with a guy I coach. I've been working with him on and off for three years. We are in his office in the city, sitting down.

JUDITH   Anything else?

MYLES   Yes. I really like working with him. It's always rewarding.

JUDITH   OK. I want you to notice yourself sitting in the chair, notice your feelings, the atmosphere in the room.

MYLES   Yes.

JUDITH   And now I want you to observe yourself as if you were at the door and could see yourself in the chair. What do you notice?

MYLES   I look comfortable, at ease and also alert.

JUDITH   So you can see yourself in the chair. What I want you to do is to allow an image to come to you, an image for yourself, and allow it to replace you in the chair. [I have started laughing – no, giggling.]

JUDITH   What's happening? [There is a faint giggle in her voice too.]

MYLES   I can't tell you.

JUDITH   Why not?

MYLES   Well, not in front of these people. They'll think I am mad.

JUDITH   Too late. Tell me what the image is.

MYLES   It's a garden gnome. One of those brightly painted plaster things.

JUDITH   What do you notice about it?

MYLES   It's bright yellow and red. A red hat. And, I think he has a fishing rod. [By now most of the people in the room are laughing too.]

JUDITH   A fishing rod?

She drew out more details and then moved the conversation on.

JUDITH   How do you understand this image, your little gnome with the fishing rod? [No judgement there then]

MYLES   This is the playful part of me. It is imaginative, creative and fun. The fishing rod is about listening and understanding. I cast the line a number of times on the water, asking questions and listening. There are a few nibbles and then a bite. This is when I really begin to understand when we reach the heart of the matter.

JUDITH   And how does this serve you as a coach?

MYLES   It's about not taking myself too seriously, not trying and staying in Self Two. It also makes for a more creative space for the person I am coaching.

JUDITH   And how does this part of you, the gnome, get in the way?

MYLES   That's not immediately obvious. It could be that I can sometimes upset serious people, and there are plenty of them, by appearing frivolous. I know this can happen. I think it's also that I can sometimes use the fishing rod a little directively, that I seek for a meaning that might not be there.

The laughter had stopped at this point because it was evident that I was learning in a direct and very powerful manner.

There is an epilogue of sorts. About a week after this demonstration I was with a player who had a very stressful work life. He was in charge of a part of an organisation of many thousands of people working in an environment that was extremely political. The coaching conversation had become oppressive. I noticed that I was struggling to add any value and, to tell the truth, felt a little out of my depth (that old, familiar Self One). In the moment of noticing this I remembered the image, my garden gnome. I lightened up. I stopped the conversation. I declared I was losing the plot. So was the player, he declared. The atmosphere changed. I summarised as best I could. I asked the simplest of questions: 'I understand that this is all complex, but how do you want it to be?'. I want you to know that this was not the 'right' question. It was a question formed by a garden gnome with the intent of freeing up a conversation. And it worked.

POSTSCRIPT

Having an insight into one's inner game, one's own uniqueness with all that goes with it balanced with the skills and models of the outer game, is essential to effective coaching. Aldous Huxley understood this when he wrote: 'If you take lessons before you are well and truly coordinated you are merely learning another way of using yourself badly'. In bringing this book to a close I want to remind you of the proposition that I laid out in the second chapter:

Effective coaching in the workplace delivers achievement, fulfilment and joy from which both the individual and the organisation benefit. …

Effective coaching … requires a predominantly 'non-directive' approach, an approach that evokes excellence, in which learning is intrinsic and satisfaction derives from the pursuit and achievement of meaningful goals. This is what effective coaching can be.

Appendix 1
Counselling, mentoring and coaching

The purpose of this appendix is to attempt to satisfy the need to differentiate between some like skills. The manner in which I do so may not appeal to all and may conflict with your own understanding. So be it. I will start by trying to distinguish between counselling and coaching.

After many years of trying and many conversations I have failed to come up with a complete and watertight distinction between coaching and counselling. The core skills involved in counselling and coaching, and indeed mentoring, are very similar, if not actually the same. These are principally the skills of listening and of asking questions. They are the skills towards the non-directive end of the spectrum of coaching skills. For this reason coaching and counselling are difficult to differentiate. However, it is important to distinguish between the two as a coach is seldom qualified to operate in the domain of a counsellor or therapist and to do so is potentially dangerous. The distinction that I play out below is appropriate for coaching that takes place in the workplace. Life coaching, for example, may employ other distinctions.

I make a distinction between coaching and counselling that works for me. I have got to hold up my hand here and acknowledge that many counsellors do not like the distinction I make here, but for all that, it has a certain validity. Counselling is concerned with the individual and with the relationship between the individual and the context in which he operates: his family and community

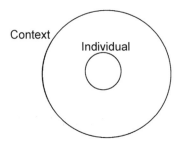

Diagram 17. The individual and the context.

(Diagram 17). Since most counselling is remedial the intent is to help the individual become 'whole' and to find their place with their family and community.

Coaching differs somewhat because it also takes into consideration the task or work that the individual is engaged in. Coaching is concerned with (a) the individual, (b) the relationship between the individual, their task or work, and (c) their context: the organisation in which the individual works (Diagram 18). The context also includes the individual's family and community, although, typically, these become a matter for discussion only if they are inhibiting performance of the task. This gives us one guideline as to what the appropriate content for a coaching session might be. A topic gets on the coaching agenda if it relates to the successful execution of the

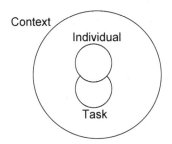

Diagram 18. The individual, the task and the context.

task. So if the player wants to talk about the squash match they had with their best friend the night before and the best friend cheated, this is probably not an appropriate topic for a coaching session – at least not one on company time.

It is probably impossible to create a complete distinction between coaching and counselling. I know that as a coach I have had conversations, appropriately, with players that a counsellor could have handled just as well. What is important is not so much the distinction between the two but to know, as a coach, when you are out of your depth, when the skill and understanding that you possess are not sufficient to support the player. Fortunately there are some checks and balances:

- A player typically reveals only what he feels safe in revealing. Most players have an intuitive sense of what is appropriate and of the skill and experience of the coach and do not cross that boundary.
- The coach equally has an intuitive sense of what is appropriate and what he is capable of dealing with.
- A well set-up coaching programme will have a clear set of goals. If the coach is concerned that the topic for a session is not appropriate then it serves both parties to ask how discussing it relates to achieving the programme goals. This helps the player to stand back and reassess.

It is likely that at some point in your life as a coach you will find yourself out of your depth, that the conversation has a strong emotional content and the player is in distress. The appropriate thing to do at this point is to stop coaching, to say explicitly that you want to end the coaching session and that you want to end it because you are out of your depth. Ask the player how they want to take the matter forward and, if possible, guide them towards counselling or therapy. Be really clear that to stop coaching does not mean that you stop listening. You need to stay with the player until they have regained sufficient composure to take the next step.

And finally to mentoring. A mentor is someone appointed or chosen to help another with the achievement of their long-term goals and career rather than immediate performance issues. The relationship is almost always outside any line-management relationship.

Appendix 2
Training coaches

There is not much available to the individual wishing to become a coach. You will find very little that is formal and organised. A brief overview reveals three loose categories of training and development activities: apprenticeship in a firm that provides coaching services, training in an allied discipline, and finally engagement with one of the few organisations offering training in coaching.

Apprenticeship in a firm providing coaching services

There is a growing number of organisations that offer executive coaching. Those that have been involved for the longest have induction and training programmes designed to support the novice through the development phases to the point where they are contributing members of staff. These programmes are typically developed within the organisation, without much reference to what might be happening in other parts of the sector, and are concerned with passing on best practice from one generation to the next. Given that most of the organisations offering executive coaching are still relatively small and the pressure to generate income is so great, it is almost always the case that the novice does not get all the attention that might be desirable and often gets pushed before the client prematurely. Nevertheless I think it is fair to say that, to date, this has been the most effective route to becoming a professional coach.

Training in an allied discipline

Many of those now operating as coaches have taken a sideways step from an allied discipline such as psychology or psychotherapy. In this category I also include other disciplines and approaches that are less recognised such Neurolinguistic Programming, Transformational Technology and The Inner Game, to name but a few. All of these disciplines have much to offer to the executive coach. But a word of warning; none of these disciplines is coaching in and of itself. I say this because many appear to believe that their discipline is coaching while the original models and approaches were developed with a different intent from coaching. You only have to look at the length – a year in some cases – of the executive coaching engagements recommended by many of the psychologically based approaches to see that.

That said, a strong background in the disciplines mentioned above, and others, should provide a very strong foundation for developing as a coach, since many of the skills acquired can transfer easily. More than that, the original discipline will offer additional opportunities; a psychologist or psychotherapist will recognise much more quickly when an individual has 'deeper' needs that cannot be met by coaching.

Formal programmes

Formal programmes are very few. This is not surprising as the market is still so small. These are programmes offered by organisations that are aimed at developing coaches or coaching skills on a commercial basis. In a few cases the organisations have developed relationships with universities and other establishments that provide various forms of accreditation. What is on offer is very broad in terms of quality and in terms of programme duration, which can be anything from two days to a year. In almost all of these cases the shape of the programme is dictated much more by what the providers believe the market will buy and much less by what is required to develop a competent coach.

Within each of these categories you will find varying degrees of professionalism, understanding of the topic and associated issues and comprehensiveness in the training. This is inevitable. However, as the profession of coaching emerges and as coaching's place in the line-manager's role is better understood there will be increasing need for consistency and quality in the training process. The remainder of this appendix describes what I believe to be the key elements of an effective process for developing competent coaches.

Development programmes: the process

My instinct is to describe what might be learned before I describe how it might be learned. But because coaching is, to quote Tim Gallwey, author of *The Inner Game of Work*, 'an art that must be learned mostly from experience', I will describe the process first. And as I think more about it, this has an inherent integrity in that a programme in which the process has precedence – comes first – is much more likely to meet the real needs of the participants and more accurately reflects the nature of non-directive coaching.

The most effective training programmes, I believe, should have three phases: Training, Apprenticeship and Supervision. Before describing these phases I would like to flag up the notion of pre-qualification – that it might be worth putting candidates through an assessment process prior to the development programme itself. This should ensure that there is a real understanding of the candidates' needs and the likelihood of their success in the programme.

The training phase. Despite my preference towards a non-directive style in the early part of the development programme, there is a place for something a little more directive. Experience does suggest that there are some models and practices that are useful and that can be quickly assimilated. However, the sooner the trainer can return to following the interest of the participant, having made some input, the better. In this phase the trainer might think of themselves as a guide more than anything else. This suggests that the guide has been through the territory before and therefore has some useful information and experience, but that the exact path is of the participant's choosing.

The purpose of the training phase is to give the participant the core models, for instance the GROW model which is familiar to many, and to develop the core skills, such as listening and asking questions, so that they can begin to coach others. A typical approach at the School is to describe a model or skill and then demonstrate it. The participants then practise the model or skill with each other and receive feedback from the programme leader and their colleagues. I refer back to the Gallwey quote above; people learn coaching by doing it and 80 percent of any programme should be focused on practice.

At the School we advocate starting with 'practice clients'; these are people who have a real need and desire to be coached but who understand that the coach is in training – the nearest thing to a 'safe environment' in the real world. This is a marvellous technique for accelerating learning and meeting the issues that the 'real world' throws up before actually being exposed to paying clients.

Apprenticeship. There may not be a very significant distinction between this phase and supervision in terms of practice. In both cases the coach is delivering coaching, possibly with paying clients, but in the apprenticeship phase it is clearly acknowledged that the coach is still learning, typically in the care of a more experienced coach and mentor. This is a more active and structured relationship then supervision with a lot of attention focused on thinking through meetings, etc., in advance. (Supervision tends to be more concerned with learning from events that have occurred.) In this phase the trainee coach also learns the consulting skills involved in delivering value to the client and account/client management skills.

Supervision. In a way this is beyond the confines of this appendix which is about the development of coaches. Supervision is an on-going process beginning in the apprenticeship phase and continuing throughout the professional life of the coach. The purpose of supervision is 'to ensure that the best interests of the player and the client are protected and to provide educative and restorative support to the coach'. Supervision is focused on three parties and the relationships between them: the person being coached, the client and the coach.

Appendix 3
Questions to ask a prospective coach – a buyer's perspective

With the continuing emergence of executive coaching as an option available to enhance the performance and development of, in particular, senior executives, the average buyer of such services is faced with many difficult decisions. Not least amongst these is the selection of the coach. In a market that has no regulation and no barriers to entry, anyone can establish themselves as a coach. The following questions are designed to help a buyer make an assessment of the capability of the coach.

• How do you propose to measure the success of the coaching?

Answering this question convincingly is one mark of a competent professional coach. It is true that it can be difficult to measure the success because some of the results are so personal. However, it is possible and having a set of performance goals and associated success measures is one option. These are generated between the coach and the person being coached and would ideally include input from a representative of the employer organisation (HR manager or line-manager). Such goals can be reviewed at the end of the programme. The term 'performance goals' is very specific; any coaching that does not produce a different order of result for the organisation should not be done in the organisation's time or paid for with the organisation's money. Another option is to collect feedback from colleagues before and after the coaching programme. Additionally, many organisations have performance management systems that can also be used to measure changes in performance and behaviour.

- Which party is the client, the person being coached or the employing organisation?

Many coaches with a background in, say, psychotherapy will tend to view the person being coached as the client. The implication of this is that what occurs between the coach and the player is completely confidential to those parties. I believe this is not right, at least in those situations where the employer organisation is paying the fees and the coaching is designed to help the individual achieve business goals. In such cases the organisation is the client, and has certain 'rights'. A representative of the organisation will want to know what the intended results of the coaching programme are and may want to make some suggestions. One way of ensuring that the best interests of both parties are served is, as suggested earlier, to generate a set of programme goals with the person being coached. Some of these goals are private and are kept between the individual and the coach while others are public and are passed to the individual's manager and an HR representative for input and feedback. The goals are revisited at the end of the programme. Other than this the content of all conversations between coach and player are confidential.

- Do you have supervision and if so in what form?

The notion of supervision is borrowed from the various 'helping' professions from psychology through to counselling and refers to a relationship between the professional and another, usually more experienced, colleague. The purpose of supervision in coaching is to ensure that the best interests of the individual being coached and the client organisation are protected and that the coach is supported and continues learning. Supervision helps a coach maintain perspective during a coaching programme and not get lost in, for instance, their own judgements, the organisational politics or the player's 'reality'. Very few coaches have any supervision but it is a vital ingredient in effective coaching .

• What training have you had?

The quality and depth of the training (if any) will give a strong indication of competence. There have emerged in the last few years a number of organisations that provide training for coaches. These vary significantly in quality. Effective training programmes will have a significant practical element and be of some length. Another common – and effective – training approach is a kind of apprenticeship model that the few reputable firms offer their staff. Psychotherapists who turn to coaching without taking the time to discover the differences may be doing psychotherapy in the workplace, which will have a different result from coaching. Retired managers intent on 'sharing their experience' may stifle the player and create dependence.

• What models underpin your coaching?

People come to be coaches through many routes. They come from the psychological and the psychotherapeutic disciplines. They come from pop psychology and philosophy. They come from the world of sport and the world of business. All of these can help but they are not coaching and if your prospective coach is predominantly dependent on any such model or background they may not be coaching. Coaching is something in its own right – a set of skills deployed with the intent to help another perform and learn. There is a growing acknowledgement that the most effective coaching is predominantly 'non-directive'. In this approach the role of the coach is to help the player explore a topic or issue, to gain a better understanding, to become more aware and from that state to make a better decision than they would have done otherwise. This does not mean that a coach should not have an area of expertise. Which would you choose – a coach with great non-directive skills or a coach with great non-directive skills and an expertise in your particular discipline? Clearly I would choose the latter, as long as they were capable of ensuring that their expertise did not get in the way of my learning.

• Why do you coach?

Perhaps I am too cynical but if the answer to this question is a version of 'being of service to others' then beware. Sure, that is almost certainly part of the answer but it is very seldom all of it. I am not going to suggest that there is only one legitimate reason to coach or that there are not people out there with a real desire to serve others, but most coaches that I have met are in some sense in it for themselves; they are fulfilling some kind of need. If they are not aware of their own motivation then they are incapable of rising above it and it will inevitable infect the coaching (for instance building dependency). Equally if they are unaware of their own make-up they are unlikely to be capable of fully understanding the person they are coaching.

• Do you have a coach?

It is surprising how many coaches do not have a coach. I am not suggesting that this needs to be a permanent feature in a coach's professional life, but I would be interested to know why someone who extols the value of coaching was not occasionally receiving coaching. However, not having a supervisor is a different, more serious, matter.

Appendix 4
Co-supervision exercise

The purpose of this co-supervision exercise is to ensure that the best interests of the player/subordinate and the organisation are protected, and to provide educative and restorative support to the coach/manager.

This exercise should be conducted between two trained coaches. Experience suggests that the best way of doing it is to have one coach ask all the questions of the other and then to switch roles. While it is possible to deviate from the questions this should be kept to a minimum.

Contract

Tell me how the stated purpose of the co-supervision exercise is relevant for you now?

Tell me what you would like to achieve in this session (additionally or more specifically)?

Tell me what your expectations are concerning confidentiality?

Tell me anything else you need to say or do to be fully present?

Focus on the coach

Tell me what I need to know in order to understand you, at this time?

Tell me how that (the above) might impact your coaching?

Tell me about anything else that you think might be relevant to this session?

Focus on the coaching practice

Tell me what coaching you are engaged in at the moment (direct reports, others, formal, informal, individual, team)?

Tell me any concerns you have about your coaching work?

Tell me any concerns you have had over the past three months?

Focus on a case

Tell me which coaching relationship/case would be most useful to focus on?

Tell me what I need to know about that?

Tell me about the contract you have with the player/subordinate (e.g. goals, ground rules)?

Tell me what you find most difficult in this case?

Tell me what you feel about the player/subordinate?

Tell me what you think about the player/subordinate?

Tell me what I need to know about the relationship between you and the player/subordinate?

Tell me what your principal strategies are in working with this player/subordinate?

Tell me how you are delivering value to the organisation?

Focus on the coach – follow-up

Tell me, as a result of this session, what you need to do for the player/subordinate?

Tell me, as a result of this session, what you need to do for the organisation?

Tell me, as a result of this session, what you need to do for yourself?

Completion

Tell me in what way I may have influenced this session?

Tell me how I could have been a more effective co-supervisor?

References and further reading

The Inner Game of Tennis by W. Timothy Gallwey
The Inner Game of Work by W. Timothy Gallwey
Emotional Intelligence by Daniel Goleman
Flow and the Psychology of Happiness by Mihaly Csikszentmihalyi
A Brief History of Everything by Ken Wilber
A Different Drum by M. Scott Peck

Index

About TEXERE

TEXERE, a progressive and authoritative voice in business publishing, brings to the global business community the expertise and insights of leading thinkers. Our books educate, enlighten, and entertain, and provide an intersection where our authors and our readers share cutting edge ideas, practices, and innovative solutions. Texere seeks to cultivate, enhance, and disseminate information that illuminates the global business landscape.

About the Typeface

This book was set in 10/14 Bembo. This typeface was modelled on types cut by Francesco Griffo in Venice in 1495 for the book *De Aetnea* by Pietro Bembo, which dealt with his visit to Mount Etna. It is considered one of the first of the old style typefaces, that were used as staple text types in Europe for 200 years. Stanley Morison supervised the design of Bembo for the Monotype Corporation in 1929. It has well-proportioned letterforms, functional serifs, and lack of peculiarities. The italic is modelled on the handwriting of the Renaissance scribe Giovanni Tagliente.

For further information contact:
www.downeycoaching.com
www.theschoolofcoaching.com